ALPHA AND OMEGA

A Study in the Theology of Karl Barth

ALPHA AND OMEGA

A Study in the Theology of Karl Barth

by

ROBERT W. JENSON

Wipf and Stock Publishers
150 West Broadway • Eugene OR 97401

Wipf and Stock Publishers
150 West Broadway
Eugene, Oregon 97401

Alpha and Omega
A Study in the Theology of Karl Barth
By Jenson, Robert W.

ISBN: 1-59244-007-X
Publication date: July, 2002
Previously published by Thomas Nelson & Sons, 1963.

TO

Blanche

PREFACE

An ancestor of this study was submitted as a dissertation to the theological faculty of the Ruprecht-Karl University in Heidelberg, Germany. Professor Dr. Peter Brunner and Professor Dr. Edmund Schlink, who reported the dissertation to the faculty, deserve the author's sincerest gratitude.

Professor Brunner, who was my "doctor-father," has become for me an ideal of precision and theological conscientiousness. Those who know his thought will recognize my debt to him. He has given generously of time, help, and patience. I am continuously grateful for the circumstances which led me to a man of such scholarship, churchly responsibility, and personal concern.

Professor Dr. Karl Barth's kindness to and freedom with younger scholars who seek his counsel is such that it is difficult to retain objectivity in writing about him. To him and to his assistant, Fräulein Dr. Charlotte von Kirschbaum, I give my thanks.

Quotations from Barth's *Church Dogmatics* are used by permission of T. & T. Clark, Edinburgh. Citations from the *Church Dogmatics* are made as follows: The first page number given is that of the German original edition; the page number of the English edition is given following a semicolon. In a few places an entire section of a volume, with the same number in the German and English editions, is referred to by using the symbol # (e.g., IV/1, #60). Any who may wish to verify or dispute an interpretation are asked to refer to the German text.

CONTENTS

ALPHA AND OMEGA

A Study in the Theology of Karl Barth

CHAPTER ONE

AN INTRODUCTORY CLICHÉ

I

"Christianity is an historical religion." This cliché of modern theology shares two characteristics with all true clichés: (1) We are all dreadfully tired of it but cannot avoid using it. (2) It is conveniently ambiguous.

The deadly inevitability of a cliché always points to a central problem and concern of the age in which it is current. The attempt to understand how Jesus Christ, a past event, can be the decisive reality in our present life is the chief problem of modern theology. To be sure, the fact that we are found by God through His action in history is no new discovery of modern times. To believe is to find the excuse and purpose of my life in a reality separate from myself. The Gospel has always proclaimed that this reality is Jesus, "crucified under Pontius Pilate." But the distinguishing characteristics of modern attempts to understand the faith appear when we try to make clear to ourselves *how* this event of antique history can be the goal and justification of life.

Classical theology [1] answered this question by describing a unique relation between the historical event of Jesus' existence and timeless realities standing triumphant above the one-thing-after-another of human history. Goodness, Beauty, Truth, and the "Being" of which these were aspects—these were in the beginning, granting solidity to the seemingly fleeting life of man, they would be in the end, guaranteeing that we were indeed get-

[1] This vague term lumps patristic, medieval, and Protestant scholastic theology together. Barbaric, but it will answer our purpose.

ting some place, and always they enfolded and protected man, giving meaning to life and providing norms for its decisions and actions.

The Church did not need to convince men of the reality of such timeless entities; they were the foundation of human endeavor, the basic stock of common sense, proclaimed equally by Plato, Jefferson, or the humblest preacher. The bedrock of reality was for all premodern culture just that—bedrock. Against eternal justice, the decisions of life could be measured, found wanting or adequate and in either case anchored. Wherever beauty was found, the shadow of a reality not subject to the change and decay of time could be seen. And whatever truth man might attain was raised from being a collection of facts into the unity of truth.

The Church could say: "The goodness which you seek is found in obedience to Jesus Christ. The truth about yourselves and your world is found in His word. Beauty is conformity with Him. In Him the eternal foundation of life has come close to us and been made real and concrete." Classically, the Church has exhibited the saving character of the history of Jesus by describing it as the place where man, who lives in time, might be united with nonhistorical timeless realities for which he already sought. Thus man might attain perfection and immortality, all that was hidden by time.

Within this broad schema a vast number of variations are possible. The precise nature of the relation between Christ and the superhistorical can be most variously described. Truth or beauty or goodness may each be emphasized above the others. All the possibilities of true doctrine and of heresy can be and have been stated in its terms. There was mystical, penitential, and sacramental theology. There was genuinely evangelical theology. The talk of "Christian ideals" and "religious values" is the last pitiable trickle of this grand tradition. And, so long as man lived in a world which thus reached from time into the timeless, it was indeed to this man that the Gospel had to be made understandable. Therefore it was within this schema that the Church had to think.

We no longer live in this framework. In our world we say of truth that it all depends on the point of view, of beauty that we don't know much about art but do know what we like, of goodness that we must each find his own values. Ours is a world in which a popular magazine has held a symposium for the purpose of *inventing* a national goal for America. The basic fact of our lives is that we do not live from day to day over against a timeless structure of reality, sustained and judged by unchanging certainties. There is no need to elaborate upon this commonplace observation, or to attempt to substantiate it.[2] Every television philosopher laments the loss of "values." [3] Nor is there any need to decide whether the disappearance of the timeless is a catas-

[2] A documentation of this claim would be simply a bibliography of contempory philosophy, political theory, and aesthetic criticism. Let me nevertheless name some studies not usually mentioned in this context and readily available: Eliade, *Cosmos and History;* Poulet, *Studies in Human Time;* Auerbach, *Mimesis.*

[3] There is a magnificent cartoon strip by George Feiffer on this subject. The drawing is the same in each of the five panels: a man seated before a television set. In each panel he makes one remark: (1) "The cultural programs on Sunday television are really great." (2) "First there is the All-Star Theology Hour. Each week a famous theologian appears and tells us that what our society lacks is religious values." (3) "Then there is the All-Star Philosophy Hour. Each week a great philosopher discusses the problems of our age and tells us how we lack ethical values." (4) "Then there is the All-Star Psychology Hour. Each week an eminent psychologist diagnoses the crisis of our time as a lack of meaningful interpersonal relationships." (5) "Then I watch Maverick."

trophe, a boon, or neither. The Church must always simply speak of Christ to man as it finds him. Since the middle of the nineteenth century (later in America?) the Church has found man forlorn in history, awaiting from its succession of events only that they shall lead to yet other events. Perhaps he has been optimistic, perhaps pessimistic, but in neither case a believer in the old gods of timelessness. But how does one exhibit, to *this* man, one of these events as finally decisive for all his days and weeks?

The old method of exhibiting the historical event of Jesus as the object of faith has become impossible to continue. It is this crisis which has made the sentence "Christianity is an historical religion" into a cliché and a symptom. For theology is thus thrown back upon history, upon the flux of time, *in itself*. The preacher must, if he is to be understood, exhibit the events of 4 B.C. to A.D. 30 as containing the meaning of his hearers' lives without recourse to sources of meaning above time, without assuming that his hearers already suppose they *ought* to reflect justice and beauty in their lives. He must exhibit Jesus Christ, "crucified under Pontius Pilate," this personage of long ago, as himself, in his own unadulteratedly temporal reality, the sole meaning of human history, of each of our histories. He must show the meaning which life has, not in itself and not in atemporal abstractions, but in Jesus the Christ.

Mid-nineteenth-century speculative and revivalist theology [4] was the last attempt to evade this challenge, "liberalism" the first attempt to face up to it, and faith in "religion" the bankruptcy of that first attempt. This study will present the thought of Karl Barth as a grandiose and pioneering answer to this challenge.

[4] From which most of the allegedly "conservative" theology of today derives.

II

"Christianity is an historical religion." As cliché this assertion is not only symptomatic in its inevitability, it is also ambiguous. When we use it we are asserting a number of different things and the convenience of the saying is precisely that it absolves us from formulating these clearly and distinctly.

There are at least three different assertions confusedly present in our platitude: (1) We are asserting that human history is the field in which God is at work to make Himself present to us, and that therefore He controls it to His purposes. That is to say, we assert that there is a "history of salvation" at the center of history. (2) We are asserting that God himself is not atemporal but in some sense is really involved in time, that He "has" a history. (3) We are asserting something about the final nature of reality, that we must look, not to the timeless, but to history, to discover it.

These three assertions may well prove to be most intimately related. Indeed, it should be plain that they are simply the various sides of the same attempt to describe how life finds its meaning in Jesus. But the cliché–character of the undifferentiated assertion is that it relieves us of the hard labor involved in understanding each of the individual assertions and the precise nature of their relation. For it is plain that when once we disentangle them and set them down clearly they raise problems of the most difficult sort.

It is the conviction behind this book that the most profound attempt yet proposed to deal with these problems may be derived from the thought of Karl Barth. In the next three chapters we will therefore direct three questions to him: (1) To what end does God rule human history, and what is the course of the history of salvation? (2) In what sense does God have a history, and what is the relation between this history and ours? That is, *how* does God guide human history? (3) What is the reality to which talk in the Church bears witness? Our task is not, therefore, to expound a particular locus of Barth's thought, but to extract from him answers to certain key questions of theology.

III

It is a further conviction behind this book that in approaching Barth in this way we do him no violence but rather help to make a unified grasp of his theology possible,[5] even though this way of setting the problem is perhaps not one that he would choose. Indeed, the hope of presenting a description of Barth's thought which is at once true to his pattern of thinking and yet more than a mere chapter-by-chapter summary of the *Church Dogmatics* is the basic motive of this analysis.

[5] The proof of this statement can only be the work itself. But some defense of it can be made. The course of the study will show that all motifs we will follow come together in Barth's christological doctrine of election. This doctrine has been authoritatively held to be the center of Barth's thought:

Berkouwer, *The Triumph of Grace* (p. 99): "[This doctrine] brings us not only to the heart of Barth's doctrine of election but also to the heart of his entire dogmatic vision."

Gleoge, *Zur Prädestinationslehre Karl Barths* (p. 194): "Karl Barth's doctrine of election is the key to his dogmatics."

von Balthasar, *Karl Barth* (p. 187): ". . . the heart of the Barthian theology."

Bouillard, *Karl Barth* (vol. 2, p. 26): ". . . the basic plan of all Barth's thought."

The celebrated feat of Hans Küng (*Rechtfertigung*) in showing that Barth's doctrine of justification could be interpreted as agreeing with Küng's version of Roman Catholic doctrine rests in fact on far-reaching agreement at just this point. (See to this: Peter Brunner, *Trennt die Rechtfertigungslehre die Confessionen?* and *Rechtfertigung und Kircheneinheit.*) Indeed, Küng's book is at least as concerned with our problem area as with the doctrine of justification as such.

Such an attempt to grasp Barth's theology in its entirety is desperately needed, especially in the English-speaking world; for I am convinced that Barth's thought is a watershed in the history of theology, that discussion must now be pursued for or againt Barth, and that a theological position must now be dated before or after Barth. Ignorance of the central core of Barth's thought dooms any contemporary theologian to obsolescence even before he begins to speak.

Yet knowledge of Barth by hearsay and from fragments is often characteristic of us. We know of him as the great overthrower of liberalism, yet are quite unaware of the very subtle character of his relations to his liberal fathers. We think vaguely of a "back to the Bible" theologian, and fundamentalist groups send their students to Basel where they are rudely awakened. We pick a few tags and labels, "Christomonism" for example, deduce from them what Barth must think—and confidently polemicise against nonexistent "Barths." Nor have we been fortunate in our translations. Until the publication of the book by Hans Küng, all the best monographs remained untranslated; and the English translation of his definitive work, the *Church Dogmatics,* is discouragingly uneven.

There is some excuse for this situation. The sheer bulk of the *Church Dogmatics* is enough to frighten anyone. Moreover, Barth's productivity has covered a long period and is by no means monochrome, thus it offers a standing temptation to seize some one segment and treat it as the whole. This temptation is also encouraged by a basic characteristic of his way of thinking. He thinks in layers or circles of reflection. What in one train of thought is a single determinant, indicated by a single concept, will appear in the next train of thought as a whole dialectical field within which some of the determinants of the first reflection may well reappear, but now on a new level. Then a third train of thought will encompass both. It is not surprising that this ferociously consistent thinker has sometimes appeared to be confusing and even self-contradictory.[6]

Nevertheless we must try. We cannot ignore the most impressive attempt yet to master the theological problems of our time. This study hopes to make a contribution to such a unified understanding of Barth.

[6] This is the weakness in many studies of Barth. The critic who seizes him by the top layer finds him a slippery customer.

CHAPTER TWO

CHRIST THE OMEGA

What was God's plan for His creation? As He led and leads it through that enigma which we call history, what is He doing with it? And if we say, as we must, that God's plan has Christ's coming in humility and glory as its center, in what sense is this true? What plans and deliberations of God led up to Bethlehem and Golgotha?

If we answer without special deliberation, if we give the first answer that comes to mind, we will probably say something like this: God decided to create a world. We really have only the vaguest idea why, but whatever the goals for His creation were, they were to be realized either in the creation as He made it, or as its natural development. To this end He then guided His creatures' history. But alas, a catastrophe occurred; the creature rebelled and God's plan was threatened. God was forced to take counsel with Himself. He had to decide whether or not to go on with His plan for the creation and if so what steps to take to get things moving again. His decision was to send His Son as a man to restore order and to open the way for the realization of God's original plan, whatever that was to be.

This answer would infuriate Barth. He charges that it makes of God's grace "a wretched expedient of God in face of the obvious failure of a plan in relation to man which had originally had quite a different intention and form. . . ." (IV/1, 68; 64)

Barth's own view is the precise reversal of this unconsidered answer of ours—as a whole and in all its parts. The task of this chapter is to expound this.

Creation and Reconciliation

Why did God create the world?

I

Not for the fun of it. That is, He did not create for the sake of creating. The creature does not exist for its own sake. It does not have its reason for existence within itself. Whatever I may be in myself, wise or foolish, rich or poor, believing or godless, none of these is my reason for being here. (III/1, 103–5; 94–6)

Why then did God create? Out of love. But love is only real in the act of loving. God wants the creature for the sake of what He, in His *grace,* intends to do with and for him. (III/1, 63; 59) The creature is there for the sake of the act of love which God intends to perform upon it. The creature is the *presupposition* of that act of love, the presupposition of the "covenant," of the relation of active love into which God intends to enter with it.

Therefore Barth's dogmatic definition reads as follows: "Creation is the . . . external basis of the covenant. . . . It prepares . . . the sphere in which the institution and history of the covenant takes place . . . the subject which is to be God's partner in this history. . . ." (III/1, 107; 97) The fact *that* the creature is and *what* it is are simply and solely the necessary preparation for its being in covenant with God. (III/1, 105–6; 96–7) If God is to perform acts of love on the creature, if He is to live in covenant with it, the creature must exist. Therefore God created it.

But now we must be careful. This does not mean that a capacity for God's love is built into the creature, so that in addition to its other characteristics it also has this one. (IV/1, 54; 51f.) The creature's destiny to live in loving fellowship with God is not discoverable by any amount of examination, empirical or philosophical. Let an omniscient psychoanalyst, an eschatological physicist, and Heidegger himself combine their efforts. They may discover my Oedipus complex, the complete mechanism of my life and my capacity for self-transcendence. But in the infinitely long final report of their investigations this one proposition will not occur: This being is created to be loved by God.

The home of this destiny is not in anything that the *creature* is. It is in the continuity of *God's* acts, in the fact that *God's* act of creation is continuous with His acts of covenant love. (III/1, 63–75; 59–69) God has done and does many things in pursuit of one purpose. It is in this unity of God's acts that the creature *is* the one destined to be loved by God.

Barth's exegesis of the biblical account of the seventh day of creation (in the priestly record) is especially illuminating in this connection. (III/1, 240–58; 213–28) God's "rest" on that day was not inactivity. On the contrary it was the act in which He exercised His eternal divine Being, His freedom and love, *as an event within the history of the creature.* (III/1, 244; 216) It is therefore the foundation of the covenant history, of that history which God and His creature *share.* (III/1, 245; 216f.) From this point on, the entire history of salvation unrolls with absolute necessity; the basic decision, that God shall be God and man man together with each other, has been made. (III/1, 244; 216)

The crucial point for our present discussion is that this first act of the history of the covenant is at the same time the last act of the history of creation. The founding event of the covenant history is the crowning event of the creation. (III/1, 245–6;

216–8) It is, indeed, constitutive for the reality of the creature that God willed to coexist with Him and that in the event of that seventh day He made himself the God who coexists with His creature. (III/1, 244; 216)[1]

Note well, nothing is created in this seventh day. Creation is finished, the creation history is not. At the end of the six days the creatures are there, but the act which makes them be there is not over. (III/1, 240; 213) The creature was produced in six days, yet it is only the work of the seven days which is in fact the creation, that is, which is the outer basis of the covenant. (III/1, 254; 224f.) That the creature is really creature, that it has the destiny of living in covenant with God, does not reside in the creature but in the continuity between that act of God in which God created it and the act of divine condescension, of covenant history. (III/1, 247f.; 219)

The creature exists because it is destined to be loved by God. It is so destined not in that it possesses certain characteristics, not in that it is loveable or needy or responsive, but in that God who makes it exist does so in an act which is continuous with His acts of love. One more step remains. The historical continuity of creation and covenant is *not* that of an historical development. (IV/1, 519; 466f.) In His eternal decree God decides to love the creature and make covenant with him; therefore He decides to create him. The unity of God's one eternal decision is the sole locus of the unity of creation and covenant. Therefore it is the sole basis of the creature's existence. (III/1, 44–50; 42–8)[2]

Thus Barth can describe the act of creation as a carrying out of God's decision before all time, His decision to *love* man. Before all time God chose to be merciful. By so doing He rejected all

[1] See also III/1, 259–62; 229–32.
[2] See below.

mercilessness. (II/2, 152; 141) He said "Yes" to one possibility and (in order to say the "Yes") "No" to all others. In his great exegesis of the first chapter of Genesis (III/1, 107–240; 98–213) Barth sees the act of creation as again such a great dividing: of the created from the not-created, of the willed from the rejected. God chooses the ordered world and rejects the chaos which might have been. God chooses the light and rejects the darkness which might have been. God chooses the land and rejects the flood.

It is the creature's good which is chosen and an evil is rejected against which the creature would have been defenseless in its own power. Creation is, therefore, the first act of God's mercy. It is the *rescue* of the creature from chaos. And so a world is created whose subsequent history can only consist of new confirmations of the original dividing of order from chaos. A world is created in which existence can only mean participation in an unshakable primal victory of light over darkness. (III/1, 130f.; 117–9) The creature exists as the first step in the fulfillment of God's one eternal decree of love.

II

To this point we have spoken of "covenant" and "love" in more or less general terms. But the covenant we know and live in is God's fellowship with *sinners,* a covenant of reconciliation based on forgiveness. (III/1, 53f.; 50) Is this the covenant which Barth calls the goal of creation? Yes. The creation is not the making possible of a covenant in general, but of the covenant of grace; the creation exists as the necessary apparatus for the reconciliation of sinners. In speaking of "creation" and "covenant" Barth means the life we now live, with its food and drink, its sins and joys, of the forgiveness we live by, and the prayers we offer.

To make this concrete, let us look at a particular section of Barth's doctrine of creation, one that is also important in other connections. In the section on "Creation as Justification" (III/1, 418–76; 366–414) Barth is concerned to show how God's act of creating justifies itself, how the world just as it really is can be seen as having an excuse for existing.[3]

God justifies the creature in view of its destiny. The world is good just as it is because it is the suitable object of God's covenant work. Precisely for this reason it has its good points *and* its bad ones, a light side *and* a shadow side. Created life rejoices *and* suffers, triumphs *and* fails, has limitless possibilities *but* is never perfect. And when God looks at His creature and pronounces it good, when He declares that its existence is justified, this includes both sides. (III/1, 422–30; 369–75) For by affirming both sides of the creature's existence God reveals that His final intention for His creature requires a double determination: it must be worthy, and it must be needy. The creature must have a light side to be worthy of fellowship with God. But it must also have a shadow side. It must also be needy, in order that in this fellowship it be completely dependent on God's mercy—indeed, on His work of reconciliation.

"Since everything is created for Jesus Christ and His death and resurrection, from the very outset everything must stand under this twofold and contradictory determination. It is not nothing but something; yet it is something on the edge of nothing, bordering it and menaced by it, and having no power of itself to over-

[3] Remember that within III/1 the theme is primarily God's *creating;* it is his own act of creating the kind of world He did which God's affirmation of the creature justifies.

come the danger." (III/1, 430f.; 376) This shadow, this weakness, this fallibility and imperfection of the creature, is not evil or sin. Nor would it have *had* to be the sign of the creature's sinfulness. But in fact, since the creature is fallen, the shadow side is the sign within the creature's good, created nature that it is fallen. It is the created mark of the creature's need of redemption.[4]

Thus God confirms creaturely existence in both its good and not so good sides as the suitable object of His purpose for it, of the work of reconciliation. It is both worthy and needy thereof. "In the interests of this divine conflict and victory [over it's imperfection] it may be imperfect. . . ." (III/1, 441; 385) The creature is created as the threatened creature in order to be the suitable recipient of grace. (And God is justified in so creating the creature because He grants this grace and has decreed it as the prior goal of all his works.)[5] In short, the world is created as

[4] For the puzzled, let us pause a little longer by this ontology of the two sides of created existence. The creature is created as the creature who left to himself must become the fallen creature—it is this which becomes visible in the "shadow-side" of his nature. The creature, however, is not left to himself. But what is the help he receives? We have just heard it is reconciliation, but that means restoration from fallenness! To understand this remarkable dialectic requires material which will be discussed in the next section on the doctrine of evil. But the distinction introduced in the text will help some: The shadow side is *factually but not necessarily* the created exponent of the creature's fallenness. It is the expression in existence of the fact that the creature is always, as soon as he himself acts, the fallen creature. "The time or 'era' of this beginning is the pre-historical era in which strictly speaking—and the saga confines itself to this—the question can only be of God's permission and command and not of the corresponding activity and existence of the creature. . . . When the creature *is* . . ., when its history as such commences . . . , the intervening regulation [the fallen state] also begins. . . ." (III/1, 238f.; 211) Thus, in *fact,* the shadow is identical with the sinfulness because of which man is "needy" for redemption.

[5] Again for the puzzled, a more complete development of this argument: God confirms creaturely existence in both its aspects, as the worthy and needy object of reconciliation. So far so good. But how can this confirmation

the suitable "arena, instrument and object of God's living action, of the once for all divine contesting and overcoming of its imperfection. . . ." (III/1, 441; 385) God has created the world in order to have an object to reconcile. The love of sinners is the reason for creation.

"And the whole cosmos was . . . created that . . . man might be what he is by the grace of God and for the grace of God." (III/1, 72; 67)

History and Reconciliation

I

The history of man begins (in the most fundamental sense possible) as a progress toward the reconciliation of sinful man in Jesus Christ. How does it continue? Barth answers as unequivocally as possible:

---

of both sides of created life reveal its perfection? Perhaps God has made the world so, but how can it be *right* that it is so? How is God *good* in all this? God's confirmation is not the solidification of the two sides but their relativizing. He confirms and surpasses the lament of the creature in order to eliminate it. He fights against his creature's imperfection; this fight is the justification of created life. In brief, the creature is allowed to be imperfect for the sake of the divine conflict and victory over its imperfection. (III/1, 441; 385) It is *this* coordination of the two sides of existence which makes the world good. The dialectic of this section is both brilliant and difficult, resulting from the interplay of two motifs: (1) God has created the world imperfect for the sake of a perfect overcoming of the imperfection. (2) He seeks to overcome the imperfection for the sake of the threatened creature. What does the "may" mean (in the passage quoted from III/1, 441; 385)? That the imperfection of the world is there for the sake of its overcoming and so is allowable? Or that the imperfection is overcome and so not fatal? Both. Two questions are asked: How does it happen that the creature is threatened with destruction? And how is this right? The first is answered: In order to be the suitable recipient of grace. The second: Because grace is given.

It is the execution of the election of grace resolved and fulfilled by God from all eternity. . . . It is the history in which God establishes His fellowship with man, and prepares and accomplishes its completion in His own self-giving to human nature and existence . . . the meaning of the continued existence of the creature, and therefore the purpose of its history, is that this covenant will . . . have its course. . . . There is no other meaning or purpose in history. (III/3, 41; 36)

He asserts that everything in that reality which is different from God, including all that happens in the freedom of the creature, serves *this* meaning. He asserts that this is the sole meaning of its continuing existence. (III/3, 41; 36) Here a distinction is made. Within the whole history of the creature there are some events especially chosen to be the history of God's covenant work. (III/1, 42; 36) But we can also abstract from this special direction by God; we may look at the history of the creature in itself, as the free activity of the life given in creation. (III/3, 43; 37f.) It is this that we ordinarily mean when we speak of "history" and it is with this that we will be concerned in this section.[6]

Of human events in this ordinary sense Barth says:

They take place as they have a part in the history of this covenant. They take place for the sake of this history. . . . They have no significance or value apart from God's covenant will and work. . . . They do not have their purpose or goal in themselves or apart from the purpose and goal to which the covenant work of God hastens. They can only hasten with it in the one direction. (III/3, 41f.; 36)

It is important to see the size of the assertion Barth makes here. The choice of a breakfast cereal—and the movements of the

[6] We will take up God's special covenant history in the next sections. It is sufficient to point out here that, as follows from Barth's doctrine of creation, the history of the covenant of grace is, from beginning to end of creaturely activity, also taking place. (III/3, 104; 92)

Communist armies—all take place solely insofar as they serve the movement of the special history of grace. Barth does not say that this meaning can be read off from the events of history. But he does say that this is the only meaning they have and that if it were not for a hidden connection with God's plan to reconcile sinners, these events would not take place.

The doctrine of "providence" has therefore a specific content for Barth which it otherwise often lacks. By "providence" we usually mean that "God will make everything work out for the best," with no clear idea of what we mean by "best." There is no such vagueness for Barth. "Providence" is the name for the fact that God orders whatever His creatures do in their freedom to the course of His covenant work.

This means that the creature as a truly free and acting subject becomes a partner in God's covenant work. Barth does not mean this in any ambiguous or over-subtle fashion. *I* do things, which I and nobody and nothing else do and which I do not have to do, which I do only because *I* and nobody else have so decided. It is *this* creature who is a partner in the covenant. And yet Barth of all people must insist that God is and remains the only subject of His covenant work.

We encounter here one of the classic problems of theology. Barth uses the following distinction. The creature is partner in the covenant, and partner as a freely acting subject, yet not as subject of the *covenant* but of his own free creaturely history.[7] It is this history in its full reality, the free subjectivity of the creature

[7] In passing: The importance of this distinction for understanding Barth can hardly be overestimated. Both Balthasar and Bouillard seem to have missed it. This has had important consequences for Balthasar's interpretation of Barth's understanding of creaturely freedom. It leads him to assert that Barth ought logically to teach the Catholic *cooperatio* and is prevented only by his tie to Protestant doctrine.

included, which God orders to His covenant purposes. (III/3, 43–53; 38–46)

Barth's comprehensive statement of the relation between creaturely history and the history of the covenant thus comes to be an exact complement to his formula for the relation between creation and the covenant. Just as created being is the "outer basis" of the covenant, so the history of created being is the "outer basis" for the history of the covenant. (III/3, 43–53; 38–46)

By this Barth means that the function of the creature's free history, of his decisions to make war, go to bed early, or marry for money, is service—service to God's loving covenant activity. It is God's tool and material in the work of the covenant. It provides time, place, and opportunity. Our history provides an historical reality with which God can make a covenant. It provides historical persons through whom He may pursue His reconciling work. In short, creaturely occurrence is the presupposition of the covenant history. God's work in which He relates Himself to creatures outside Himself requires that there *be* a reality outside Himself. (III/3, 53–6; 46–9)

Here Barth gives exactly the same warning as he did in the doctrine of creation. Our history does not have this function in itself; there is no pattern of history, no immanent laws of its working, which qualify it as servant of God's covenant. Our history has this function only in the act of God in which He uses it for this purpose. (III/3, 60; 51f.) Again, God's activity in which He uses our history for the purposes of His covenant work does not have its unity in some necessary scheme of divine activity or law of historical development but solely in the unity of His eternal decision. God's providence is therefore simply that God who created us because He had chosen to make covenant with us, *continues* to be the same God, the God who on the basis of the election of grace elects the creature to its own particular being and existence. (III/3, 81; 71)

II

The final point is that here, just as in the doctrine of creation, the goal of all God's works is not a covenant in general, but reconciliation of sinners in Jesus Christ. By way of proof and illustration, let us again choose a particular section to report more fully, the section in which Barth treats God's providence as "preservation."

Barth is as explicit as possible. "Because *servatio,* therefore *creatio,* and therefore *conservatio.*" (III/3, 91; 80) The creature, which has its being from God's division between what He wills and what He does not will, is unable in itself to preserve this distinction. It is threatened by nothingness. If left to itself it must succumb. Of its own power the creature cannot maintain that distinction between what God wants and what God does not want which is the origin of the creature's life; if left to itself the creature will always mix acts in which it affirms what God created it to be with acts in which it affirms what God created it not to be. Only God can save the creature. (III/3, 83ff.; 73ff.) For the creature is destined to take part in Jesus' victory over chaos. Its own inability to overcome chaos, its own weakness over against the threat of falling, is the necessary corresponding factor in its nature. Because the creature is permitted to *be along* at God's act of rescue and liberation, therefore it is permitted to *be* —and to be *as* a creature in that infinite danger in which it can neither protect nor preserve itself. (III/3, 91; 80) The creature's destiny is to live entirely from grace—and this is exactly its glory.

Thus God preserves the creature from falling into nothingness in order that the creature may be there to take part in God's victory—over the creature's fall into nothingness. Here we have the same remarkable dialectic we encountered in the doctrine of creation where Barth spoke of the "shadow side" of creation. The threat of nothingness is not the same as actual fallenness into it. That I am by myself infinitely weak in the face of temptation does not mean that I actually am what God has decreed I shall not be. For I am not left to myself; God gives the help I so mortally need. But He helps me in such a way as never to obscure my need of that help. And thus the threat of nothingness, which is not in itself the same as a fall, comes, as a factor in the history of the covenant, to stand at the point of that fallenness of man which is overcome in Christ's victory.[8]

The result: (1) The creature is preserved in order to take part in the overcoming of the empty and false life to which it, *in itself,* is forfeit. (2) The creature is preserved in the way which corresponds to this purpose.

The goal of history, all history, is the victory of the covenant of grace in Jesus Christ.

Nihility

We have been working point by point through the unreflected position we made the basis of discussion. And we have arrived at the following point: "But alas, a catastrophe occurred; the creature rebelled and God's plan was threatened." The perverse reality thus described has already introduced itself several times in our discussion. It is now time to ask what evil *is* in Barth's system. How does Barth at *this* point understand God's decision

[8] See the whole discussion of God's substitutionary intervention for us on pp. III/3, 92ff.; 81ff.

to be merciful as the starting point of all His ways? What place does evil have in the doing of that mercy which is the goal of all God's works?

I

To answer this question we must again go back to Barth's doctrine of God's eternal decree. We have already seen that God from all eternity chose to be the God of grace and so rejected all other possibilities, that He chose to will what He willed and by doing this, denied all else. Here is the key to Barth's doctrine of evil.

God's eternal, positive will is His will to sacrifice himself in the Incarnation of His Son for the benefit of man whom He created and who fell away from Him. (II/2, 175; 161) This choice is necessarily a *double* predestination:[9] God chose that He himself would live for man and that man would live for Him. Since man is rebellious and fallen this meant that God chose to lose in order that man might gain. For himself God chose involvement with sin and evil, since the man with whom He chose to identify Himself is sinful and evil. For man God chose blessing, fellowship with Himself, life within the richness of His own life, life as the mirror of His own blessedness. (II/2, 175–85; 161–9)

In this doubleness of God's will lies God's permission of evil. It is the necessary reverse of this good will of God. (II/2, 185; 169f.)

Because God's creation of and work with creatures, with a reality outside Himself, is based on a choice, it is always "jealous," always judging. He chooses, and therewith condemns all that He

[9] Note that Barth's "double" is quite different from that of classical Calvinism.

does not choose. That is, He is holy; as He works on and with His creatures He is asserting Himself and them against this that He rejected. Evil is this opposition to God's work. Barth calls it "nihility." [10]

It is from this negative side of God's eternal choice and the resultant negative side of all His works that nihility derives its existence—and only from there. Nihility *is* only the object of its own condemnation. In that God rejects, He rejects "something"; evil is precisely this "something." Nihility "is," therefore, in an extremely problematic fashion. It exists only as the object of the authoritative decision that it shall not exist. But in this fashion, it *does* exist. (III/3, 405ff.; 351ff.) Nihility is that which God does *not* want. It lives only from this. But it does indeed live from this. For not only God's will but also His not-will is *powerful* and cannot lack a correspondent in reality. The reality corresponding to the divine not-will is nihility. (III/3, 406; 352)

It is also from this negative side of God's eternal choice that nihility derives its nature. It is *evil.* For what God wills is mercy. What He does not will is therefore merciless. (III/3, 407ff.; 353ff.)

Only God can overcome nihility, when He carries out the work of mercy which He has decreed. His "strange" work, through which nihility achieves such existence as it has, occurs only as the reverse side of this work of grace. In that He carries grace to its goal His strange work also comes to its goal—which is precisely the destruction of nihility. For we must always remember when dealing with Barth's doctrine of evil that the will of God which calls nihility forth is exactly the same will which wills that this opposition to mercy and obedience shall *not* exist. (III/3, 406–10; 352–5)

[10] *Das Nichtige.* The published translation uses "nothingness."

Therefore nihility has no permanency. Nihility is in its very essence the eternally *past,* that which is there only as the prelude to its own disappearance. Strictly speaking it never "is." Rather we should always say: Nihility *was.* For God's strange work of condemnation is not an eternal process. As a reverse side it is unavoidable but also temporary. When He carries out His work of love, His strange work becomes superfluous and ceases—and with it its object. Of course God always remains eternally holy, eternally the judge, eternally the one who has chosen, but He is all of this most emphatically after His finished, accomplished judgment. Nihility fulfills its original destiny on Calvary; this destiny is that it ceases to exist. Once God has finished saying "No," He does not continue to say it. Then that which He denies, that which exists only as the object of His denial, ceases. (III/3, 416ff.; 360ff.)

In summary: Nihility has existence as a by-product of God's eternal decision of grace, of His decision to reconcile fallen man to Himself.

It exists only as the necessary object of its own overcoming, and it is this overthrow which is positively willed by God. (III/3, 419; 362f.) Like the creature, it exists within and because of a destiny, but its destiny is to be destroyed. "That which is eliminated"—this is both its existence and its essence, which it has only by relation to God's work of reconciliation in Jesus Christ. (III/3, 380; 331)

We have been discussing the ontology of evil, abstractly and so perhaps a bit confusingly. It is in fact difficult to say concretely what Barth means by "nihility." He does not mean the actual acts of sin which are performed by us, nor the actual evils of historical life. "Nihility" is rather the absolute negation which horrifies us when we sometimes glimpse it *through* and *in* the actual sins and evils of life. Yet to be true to Barth we must remain concrete and not wax metaphysical. Perhaps we may say: Nihility is the very concrete world of complete disorder and mercilessness which *might* have been had not God created, in Christ the reconciler, the good world which He in fact did create.

II

It is now time to move from absolute evil, from "nihility," to the more existential side of the doctrine of evil, to sin. Here we are in possession of the most precise statement we could wish: "In all its forms sin is man's perverted dealing with the stern goodness and righteous mercy of God addressed to him in Jesus Christ." This proposition belongs "to the basic substance of my dogmatics. . . ." (IV/3, 427; 369f.) Sin occurs only as a negative reaction to God's grace, to God's *forgiving* grace in Jesus Christ. (III/2, 40; 35) To anticipate formulations which have to be discussed more fully, sin is simply man's attempt to behave as if he were not reconciled to God through Jesus Christ.

Barth carries this pattern through consistently. He distinguishes and discusses three forms of man's sin. To take these in order: Man's pride (IV/1, #60) is his refusal to be saved by Jesus Christ. It is his refusal to believe that God has chosen him, his refusal to live in dependence upon this choice. (IV/1, 435f.; 393f.) Nor is this the case only for those who hear and reject Christian preaching; all sin is and always has been unbelief in Jesus Christ. (IV/1, 460; 414f.)

The same is true of man's inertia. (IV/2, #65) It is the attempt to behave as if Jesus Christ were not risen, to continue in the old ruts which sufficed before this intrusion of a new world. (IV/2, 530; 469) Man has been chosen and created to be Jesus

Christ's brother; his sin is his lazy failure to snatch the opportunity. (IV/2, 460ff.; 409ff.)

In a special sense this pattern holds for Barth's third aspect of man's sin, his untruthfulness. (IV/3, #70) Through Christ's prophetic office God attacks the world, in that He proclaims that its situation has been radically changed. This message provokes resistance, it provokes man's contrariness. Barth is very insistent that the message is the word of grace for sinners and that this message comes *before* the resistance which it attacks, that this resistance exists only as a denial of the already-spoken message. (IV/3, 281, 289f.; 245, 251ff.) Man's untruthfulness is truth's "negative mirror-image." (IV/3, 289; 251f.) Indeed, Barth develops the question of man's sin as the *negative* effect of Christ's revealing work. (IV/3, 318; 276) In sum, sin is a lack of correspondence with God's grace—to sinful man.

I think the reader may be excused some confusion at this point. Surely sin precedes the message of its forgiveness? Surely it is there before the one comes who comes to conquer it? In one sense this is, of course, true. And Barth is well aware of it. He defines sin as that which is presupposed by reconciliation in Christ, which is uncovered by reconciliation, which precedes it. (IV/2, 423ff.; 378ff.) Yet immediately upon the pages in which he does so there follow the definitions given above, where the order is the exact opposite, where grace goes before sin. To understand Barth we must therefore distinguish: Sin is the negative *pre*supposition of God's act of reconciliation in Christ, but a presupposition which exists only as the negative reaction to this very act.

Now it is not hard to understand the remarkable helplessness which Barth attributes to sin. Something which becomes real just at the point of its own defeat is not going to be creative. Sin reaches its fullest reality at the crucifixion, exactly where God uses it against itself. The very place where sin is real is the place where iron boundaries are set for it. (IV/1, 441, 452; 398f., 408)[11]

Sin lacks all creative power. It cannot produce a kingdom of its own alongside the kingdom of God the Creator and Reconciler. (III/2, 37–9; 33f.) Nor can it effectively attack God's kingdom; it cannot change the creation. For God does not cease to be God because man sins. And therefore man does not cease to be man, for his being is the destiny which God alone gives him. (III/2, 271; 227f.) Man can make himself relatively but not absolutely godless. (IV/1, 534; 480) The being of sinful man remains a being which rests on election, on God's decision that he shall be a fellowman of Jesus Christ. Sinner though he be, he exists because God calls to him in Christ. Sinner though he be, he exists in that he has a place in the history of God's work in Christ. (III/2, 170–207, 235f.; 142–74, 197f.)

And so human nature, which we saw to be man's adaptation to this destiny, can neither be destroyed nor altered by sin. (III/2, 329ff.; 273ff.) For man is from the very beginning chosen for no other purpose than to take part in Christ's victory over sin. (III/2, 170ff.; 142ff.) "Man has not fallen lower than the depth to which God humbled Himself for him in Jesus Christ." (IV/1, 534; 480f.) At the very beginning the doors were shut against all ultimate dualism, in God's eternal decision, and what God has shut is not even temporarily reopened. It has been determined from the beginning that evil can exist only within impenetrable boundaries. (IV/1, 453; 408f.)

[11] This is one point from which to grasp Barth's famous assertion of the ontological impossibility of sin. A possibility is that which can *become* real, i.e. which has a future. That which "is" only at the point of its own disappearance has no future.

III

We have heard some sizeable assertions. We have heard a conception in which God's decision to show grace comes first even in His permission of evil. God has created the world as the presupposition of His work of reconciliation. But for a work of *reconciliation* yet another presupposition seems required. Dare we summarize our present discussion of evil and sin: God permits evil as the negative presupposition of His work of reconciliation?

This is an awesome question. And the affirmative answer which seems required could, if understood in a certain way and taken seriously, give us the most sinister sort of comfort. The way in which, if at all, the question is to be answered affirmatively will be the subject of the next section. First we must show the way in which an affirmative answer is *not* to be made.

We must first be clear that according to Barth sin and evil have no basis in God's creation. "In creation as such no sin takes place and no sin is envisaged." (III/1, 238; 211) Sin is neither the work of the Creator nor an activity of the creature. It can be derived neither from the positive will of the Creator nor explained as the sole work of the creature—for the creature does nothing alone. Nor is sin part of the relation *between* Creator and creature; it is not even the boundary of this relation, but its breakdown. (III/3, 330–3; 291–4) The decision to sin is therefore not an exercise of the creature's freedom; sin is not among the possibilities of his nature among which he may choose. (III/2, 328f.; 272–4)

It is not hard to see how Barth can and must say all this, despite the conclusion to which our discussion seems to tend. The being of the creature is precisely his destiny to participate in grace; sin we have seen defined as the opposition to grace.

Sin is therefore the "ontological impossibility" of created existence. For a creature, to be is to be destined to be with God in Christ. Man's denial of God is therefore denial of himself (III/2, 162; 136) It has caused a good deal of astonishment that Barth labels sin an "impossibility." For our present purposes we may understand this label as follows: Sin has no basis in anything that is real, nor is there any basis for *its* being real. It has neither a metaphysical ground nor a possible rational explanation. (IV/1, 454; 408f.) Indeed, its very essence is just this impossibility; it is the fact which is merely fact (in sinister parody of grace, which is *pure* fact).

But what of creation's "shadow side"? By this term Barth designates the actual evils of life, its misfortunes and sufferings, and says of this shadow that it is an essential part of created life. Is not this a claim of evil in created reality and so in the positive will of the Creator? Barth denies that the shadow side of creation has as such anything to do with nihility. (III/3, 403; 350) It is part of the creature's nature, of its good nature. It is essential to the *perfection* of the creature to need its creator, for the goodness of the creature is found in its relation to reconciliation, of which its weakness and imperfection is an essential part. To be sure, the imperfections of created life remind us that the creature is threatened by nihility, indeed fallen to it, but the creature is not lost just because it has this shadow. (III/1, 435; 379–81)

Still, it is clear that there is another side to the matter. Barth is careful to say that it is the shadow side "as such" which has no connection with fundamental evil. The shadow is good because it marks the creature's dependence on reconciliation—and we remember that where the shadow side appeared as a factor in the concrete history of reconciliation it was interchangeable with man's need for forgiveness of sin. It is time to look more closely at this.[12]

Once more, what is the shadow side of creation?

Nihility is . . . not simply identical with that which *is not,* which God is *not,* which the creature is *not.* God is God and *not* a creature, but from this no nihility results in God. . . . And the creature is a creature and *not* God, but again it does not follow from this that the creature as such is marked by nihility. . . . [But] through the "not" which . . . from two viewpoints—as the creature's distinction from God and as its inner distinction [between the plurality of creatures] —belongs to the nature of the creature, that which we have called the creation's "shadow side" is constituted. On this shadow side the creature *borders* on nihility, for this "not" is the expression and so also the *boundary of God's . . . positive will* [last italics mine]. (III/3, 403; 349f.)

The shadow side of creation is that factor within the good creation which marks the fact that God's positive will to create it has a limit, a reverse, a side in which *evil* has its negated reality.

In the positive will of God as such, evil has no place. And so evil has no place in the creation, for the creation is the product of God's will. There are no direct connections between creation's shadow side and evil: The fallenness of creation does not develop out of its shadow side. Creation's fallenness is not the cause of the existence of the shadow side. The shadow side is not necessarily the created exponent of the creature's fallenness.

But "the positive will of God as such" is an abstraction. God's will is in reality *that* positive will which has a negation as its reverse. This fact must come to expression also in that which God's will creates—and does so in the shadow of imperfection

[12] In what follows I do not reproduce Barth's teaching but analyze his dialectic.

and mortality which lies over created being. Now the content of this reverse of God's will is the destruction of *evil,* and so its preliminary *existence.* Therefore the shadow side of creation, which "as such" has nothing to do with sin and radical evil, nevertheless is *factually* its created mask and representative, the sign that the creature is radically dependent on grace. (IV/1, 398; 360f.)

This leads us deeper. The shadow is the sign that the creature is created "on the edge of nihility," as the *threatened* creature. This dangerous situation of the creature must be radically understood; the creature considered in abstraction must necessarily fall. But the real creature is not this abstraction; the creature is not left to himself. The creature's very being, as we have repeatedly seen, is his destiny to be helped by God, to be saved from this threat. (III/2, 174f.; 145–7) However, now it is time to take notice of a previously unmentioned factor in this choosing and destining which constitute created being: The creatures "are not simply and directly the covenant-partners of God as his creatures; they are destined to become this." (III/2, 268f.; 225) *Within* the destining which is the creature's being and in which it is indeed secure against evil there is a movement in time and so a *"not yet,"* a time when the helpless creature *awaits* its salvation. It is plain that this "not yet" at least points to that creature in abstraction who must fall. Here is the point where the threat which belongs to the nature of the good creature and which is concrete in its shadow of imperfection can also be the creature's need of forgiveness and reconciliation. (III/3, 344f.; 303f.)

With all this not one word of what we began with has been called into question. Evil has no basis in creation. "Man cannot now appeal to his defencelessness, to the natural weakness of all being in the face of the overwhelming power of non-being. He cannot bewail and justify himself as a sinner on the ground that he is inevitably delivered up to the forces of evil." (III/2, 175; 146) But it remains also true that the creation is the fulfillment of God's eternal decree of grace—and so of *double* predestination.

We must next be clear that sin and evil have no basis in God's grace as such. Barth is aware of the possibility of confusing his position with the neo-Protestant view in which, he claims, a neat synthesis of good and evil is attempted. (IV/2, 447; 398) Here man's shame is a part of God's plan for him, a counterpart of God's majesty within a greater harmony. (IV/2, 445f.; 397f.) Sin becomes the conflict in a drama which would not be complete without it. It achieves a relative necessity in God's plan for man's development. (IV/1, 413–27; 373–87) It would not be surprising if the reader supposed that Barth said something very like this himself. But Barth vigorously maintains that all this is false doctrine and that his own view is very different.

Since sin is opposition to grace it can have no basis in it. (III/2, 40; 35) That which made Golgotha necessary is *not* willed by God. (III/3, 346; 304f.) Yet Barth concedes a remnant of truth to the neo-Protestant thesis. God is indeed Lord also of sin. It cannot compete with Him. Sin's moment of triumph is indeed just where God uses it to fulfill *His* purpose. (IV/1, 452f.; 408f.) To what, exactly, does he then object?

He objects to the postulate of a higher order in which grace and evil fit together. Salvation is no play, with a plot which encompasses both "problem" and "resolution." It is true that God stands supreme over good and evil both, but His supremacy over evil is that of His unconditional rejection. (IV/1, 453f.; 409f.) There is no positive relation between evil and grace. The use which grace makes of evil does not take place within a peaceful coordination but at the cross. God's wrath destroys the old man —and only in this way makes use of him. (IV/2, 448f.; 399f.)

He further objects to the attempt to establish a system of thought which will encompass sin as a factor. Sin has no norm. It cannot be incorporated into a system of interlocking concepts. It is the essentially lawless and irrational. It cannot be captured in thought, only overcome in action. (III/3, 408f.; 353f.)

However, to nail down the exact nature of Barth's objections and in particular to see clearly to what Barth does *not* object, we must be more detailed. For this purpose we will now examine closely Barth's critique of Schleiermacher, *the* neo-Protestant. (III/3, 365f.; 319ff.)

According to Barth, Schleiermacher asserts an *order* of sin and grace; he makes sin necessary for the sake of redemption. Grace cannot be grace without sin. Barth calls this false doctrine. Why? There are three points: (1) The real grace of God is not dependent on the presence of sin; grace which can exist only together with sin is false grace. True grace forgives and eliminates sin. (III/3, 382; 333f.) (2) Precisely because grace is the justification of the sinner, one dare not make it seem that sin is justified from the start by being necessary for grace. (III/3, 382; 333f.) (3) The relation between sin and grace is not a positive one, but a conflict between victorious grace and defeated evil. (III/3, 382f.; 333f.)

Our present concern is with what Barth does *not* deny here. He denies that grace is dependent on the presence of sin. He denies that it does not or can not eradicate sin. He does not deny that it is essential to grace to *have* once overcome sin. He denies that any system which justifies sin in advance can be correct— and denies it exactly because grace is essentially the justification of sinners. He denies that a positive relation exists between sin and grace. But he does not deny that the existence of the conflict between them is willed by God.

What does Barth object to in the neo-Protestant doctrine of evil? First, he objects to a confusion in which what exists only as the object of God's negation becomes an object of his positive will, a confusion in which God's denial—wherein sin has its reality—is seen as secretly affirmative, as a less than categorical denial of its object. His own view, that evil exists in that it is the object of God's negation *and* that this unwill is the unavoidable reverse of the choice which God has in fact made, is not touched by this objection.

Second, he objects to all attempts to make use of the unity of God's will in order to establish a synthesis of sin and grace by which we may excuse ourselves. It is *not* denied that God's "No" stands in the service of His "Yes," that God's will is one. It is not even denied that this unity is revealed to us, as the truth which uses *us*.

But we are trespassing on the next section. Again, our starting point remains; sin has no basis in grace as it has none in creation. It is not necessary.

We have now seen in what ways it may not be asserted that God permits sin for the sake of grace. Is there any way in which this *may* be said? So much is clear, and this is the conclusion of this section: Sin and evil exist in God's counsel as that which is to be overcome by reconciliation in Jesus Christ.

Contingent Reconciliation?

We have come to what is in many ways the most upsetting question of this chapter: In what sense is the coming of Christ to reconcile man God's reaction to sin? In what sense is it an expedient in view of a disturbance of God's plans? The best approach to this problem will be a presentation of the first "paragraph" of the *Church Dogmatics*' doctrine of reconciliation. (IV/1, #57)

I

"God with us" is a particular act of God and the center of all other acts by Him. Here God goes beyond the gift of being to the gift of salvation, to the gift of the fulfillment of being, of the reaching of life's goal. This fulfillment lies in fellowship with God, in participation in His life. Such a sharing in God's life is something on which the creature has no claim at all; the gift of it is grace in the strictest sense. (IV/1, 2–8; 1–9) It is this fulfillment which is primary in God's will; in order to achieve it He has created and preserved us. (IV/1, 8f.; 9f.)

"God with us" means, moreover, God with that mankind which has thrown away its salvation and endangered its being. It is the uniqueness of the event of grace that is at once a fulfillment and a rescue. Indeed, only in this way, as the overcoming of a contradiction, can it be the free grace, the *factum purum,* which it essentially is. (IV/1, 9–11; 10–12)

"God with us" means finally that God has made *himself* the rescue. He has stayed with us despite our opposition, absorbed all our wrath, made His own person the means of restoring the breach. Thus He fulfills His original will for us as well, for this will was that we should participate in Him. (IV/1, 11–13; 12–24)

"God with us" is Jesus Christ. (IV/1, 17–19; 17–19)

With this general background Barth then pursues some lines

more fully. Jesus Christ is God in His work of reconciliation. Very well. But what does "reconciliation" mean? Barth defines it as the confirmation and restoration of a fellowship which still exists but is threatened by a divisive element. At the same time it is the attainment of the original goals of that fellowship. Barth names this "original fellowship" the "covenant." (IV/1, 22; 22)

As an act of reconciliation God's will to be and remain in covenant with man conquers sin. In this victory it also fulfills and reveals itself. What is revealed is precisely the basic character of God's covenant will, that this was always God's will, that it was God's will before sin entered the picture. In the overcoming of sin the last and most extreme possibility is realized—God becomes man. Barth argues that it is impossible that this ultimate occurrence should have been a secondary factor in God's plan; as the last it must also be the first. The Incarnation is God's original plan, revealed in the event of reconciliation. (IV/1, 36f.; 35f.)

Thus God's overcoming of the contradiction of sin is characterized as faithfulness to a "previous divine decision," as the victorious continuation of an activity in which He has been engaged since the beginning. (IV/1, 37; 36) God has chosen and determined Himself from all eternity to be man for men. (IV/1, 47; 45)

Reconciliation is therefore the fulfillment in spite of opposition of an original unity of God with mankind. Of course sin is an interruption and its overcoming a contingent reaction of God. But this "reaction" occurs in the path and with the momentum of an activity of God which has been in progress since the beginning. Precisely in this special form, the overcoming of an interruption, He reveals what He has always been doing. This original unity of God with man, this original activity of God, is the "covenant." It is that which in the work of reconciliation in Jesus Christ becomes visible as the presupposition of that work. (IV/1, 37; 36f.)

What is this "covenant," this original unity of God and man? It is the fact that God has from the first not been neutral toward man. He is and has been *for* us. This is more than creation, more than preservation. In that reconciliation happens, this beneficence of God is revealed as reconciliation's presupposition and comes to its fulfillment. (IV/1, 38f.; 37f.)

This covenant is a covenant of grace. It is freely given to those who have not earned it. When we view the covenant as a covenant of reconciliation, this is obvious. Clearly, *rebellious* man has not earned God's fellowship. But that God is for us, rebellious or not, is unearned and can only be a contingent fact of God's free choice. (IV/1, 40f.; 39f.) The covenant is God's *good* deed. Again this is obvious where God must reconcile sinners. But that God is for us, sinners or not, is good—in that *He* is good. (IV/1, 41f.; 40f.)

Finally, since the "original covenant" is a covenant of grace and goodness it, like reconciliation, has its center in Jesus Christ. (IV/1, 45–8; 43–6)

What have we heard? It would seem that we have heard of a covenant which is not yet a reconciling covenant with sinners. It would seem that we have heard of a grace which is not yet forgiveness. And it would seem that it is this covenant in general and grace in general which is the original will of God. It would seem, that is, that our whole understanding of Barth has been overthrown.

The solution lies in the nature of the analysis which Barth is making here. We must observe this carefully. He does not say that such a "grace" or "covenant" has ever actually existed by itself. This covenant is what the event of reconciliation reveals as its presupposition—and that is all that it is. It is not a reality in itself. Barth is not describing an actuality but analyzing the inner dialectic of what is and always has been one event, the event of the covenant-as-reconciliation.[13] That this diagnosis is correct is proven as Barth goes on to say what the point of making this distinction is: The reason for pointing out this "original covenant" is to make clear the unconditional and eternal validity of reconciliation! (IV/1, 48; 46) The purpose is exactly the opposite from a relativizing of reconciliation, exactly the opposite from making it the contingent form of a prior and superior reality which might have taken some other form. Sin is indeed the typical "incident." (IV/1, 48f.; 46f.) Reconciliation is indeed, as it happens, God's reaction. But this does not mean that reconciliation might not have happened. The whole point of Barth's distinction is to establish this, to show reconciliation as the first work of God's right hand, to demonstrate that it is the carrying out of God's absolute and original will. (IV/1, 49; 47)

God has not become man just to get rid of hindrance, but to fulfill the original promise: "I will be your God." Jesus Christ is not only the healer of a breach but is Himself the fulfillment of a promise which antedates the breach. He is the fulfillment of a promise which antedates the historical implementation of God's will and is the basis of all God's works. (IV/1, 49f.; 47f.)

But are we not back in our quandary? Now it seems that while the Incarnation is not contingent to the events of history, its character as an act of reconciliation is. It seems that God indeed planned eternally to become man but that the concrete circumstances of Gethsemane and Golgotha were not included in the original plan. But the apparent contradiction is finally resolved when Barth continues:

[13] See also pp. 114ff., below.

It is indeed true that in the event of reconciliation God's eternal activity "takes the form" of a conflict with sin. But it is victorious in this conflict because sin is already contradicted in the eternal covenant before all time. In that this action is finished in time, sin is contradicted "also" in time! (IV/1, 50; 47f.) This is why the reconciling events in Palestine are not incidents. They are the temporal fulfillment of an "original covenant" which itself was already a covenant in spite of sin. They are the fulfillment of an eternal divine will which already had the second side in which evil exists and is overcome! "In this sense the atonement accomplished in Jesus Christ is a necessary happening. This is its unconditional validity. . . . For in Jesus Christ we do not have to do with a second, and subsequent, but with the first and original content of the will of God, before and above which there is no other. . . ." (IV/1, 50f.; 48)

At the end of it all we arrive at this: Jesus Christ, as He lived and acted in Palestine is the content of the eternal covenant. (IV/1, 57; 54) The presupposition of reconciliation is God's eternal decision, which was made before all time "exactly as it is fulfilled and revealed in time." (IV/1, 57; 54)

The point of Barth's analysis has been to establish that reconciliation through the coming of Jesus Christ as a man is its own presupposition, that within God's plan it is contingent to nothing —and yet is not arbitrary but founded in events. Reconciliation is God's reaction to sin, but that just this reaction should take place was decided before all time.

II

Finally we see what this means for the question of the previous section. Barth goes on: The fulfillment of the covenant is simply that God's promise, "I will be your God, and you shall be my people," becomes an historical event in the person of Jesus Christ. (IV/1, 71; 67) This fulfillment has the character of a reconciliation, of the restoration of an endangered fellowship. From the beginning the history of man has been the history of man's breaking of the covenant, of his rebellion against being loved. Man does not wish to live by grace alone; he insists on being something apart from God. The natural result of this would be that the covenant finally came to nothing. (IV/1, 71f.; 67f.)

The fulfilling of the covenant must therefore become a reconciling. In becoming this it assumes a radical form in which *only* God can be the one who fulfills it, in which the covenant's fulfillment becomes an *overflow* of grace. Now man has nothing more to contribute but can only receive God's love and forgiveness as an utterly inexplicable fact. He can only wonder and rejoice that God has in fact shown Himself superior also to man's rebellion and unwillingness. Grace triumphs over man and his sin, it becomes a great "nevertheless." (IV/1, 72f.; 68f.)

And so:

> Now it triumphs—in the midst of man's opposition to it—at last really wonderful, one-sided, lordly. Shall we say, "Now all the more lordly"? "Only now really working and revealing itself as completely free grace"? . . . we can and must say just that. "Where sin increased grace abounded all the more!" (Romans 5:20) It is true: What God's grace is and can do first shines forth finally and unequivocally when it shows itself to be and is active as grace for those *unworthy* of grace, grace for lost sinners. (IV/1, 73; 68f.)

To be sure, the ancient prayer which praises the *felix culpa,* the "blessed sin which merited so great atonement" is false. If virtue merits nothing from God then surely sin does not. And where God sets himself against something there is nothing *felix* about it. (IV/1, 73; 69) Here one must be very severe:

> *God's wisdom* is one thing, his wisdom which permits this incident in order to take—not it but its overcoming—as occasion to make his grace all the greater, to exert and reveal it as his *free* grace. One has to say it: Only in this overcoming is his grace so exerted and revealed as corresponds with his eternal intent and will. . . . A human pseudo-wisdom which gave out this incident as somehow necessary and so excused man . . . would be something else. (IV/1, 74; 69)[14]

The connection between sin and grace, the "in order that," lies wholly in the unity of God's great decision and can be encompassed by no human thought. This movement of God's wisdom and will is not ours to ape; the unity of sin and grace which is therein encompassed we can realize only as confession of sin, only in fleeing from our sin to the grace which is promised us. (IV/1, 74; 69f.)

But the "in order that" remains. God, asserts Barth, allows sin in order that His grace may be carried out as He has from eternity decided, as the reconciliation of sinful man through the coming of His Son Jesus Christ.[15]

Summary

We have come to the end of the substance of this chapter. We will conclude with a discussion of a classical question of theology

[14] I have retranslated this passage and that just previously quoted. The published translation contains errors at the key points in both passages.

[15] Bouillard lacks appreciation for the radicalness of Barth's thought at this point. Perhaps that is why he so often seems to be discussing Protestant theology in general rather than Barth, why so many of his very correct presentations are so curiously indecisive.

raised by it. But first it is time to remind ourselves of what we have been saying, affect a greater precision, and summarize. We have spoken of "covenant of grace," "grace," "reconciliation," and so forth as the absolute goal of all God's works. What Barth means by all such terms is the person of Jesus of Nazareth, the Christ. He means the event of his existence.

The basic element of God's eternal plan, the one goal of all His will for a reality separate from Himself, is that He should become one with sinful man in the person of Jesus Christ. This decision *is,* for Barth, the eternal decree of God. (II/2, 171; 157) Thus all the works of God are those which He does in order to carry out this decision, in order that Jesus Christ shall exist. Jesus' life is that "to which everything else is related and which everything else can only follow." (III/2, 173; 143) This self-determination of God is His free decision. This would not have had to be God's line of action. But He has in fact so chosen and is no longer separable from this His choice. (II/1, 583f.; 518–20) "The reason why God created the world and set up in it the office of reconciliation is because He was able, willing and ready to be one with the creature in Jesus Christ and because He did in fact do this." (II/1, 579; 515)

Utrum Christus Venisset, Si Adam non Peccasset?

A study of the answer given by Barth to this famous question is perhaps a little to the side of our line of inquiry, but not far. And it seems to me that there must be some readers who now wonder what his answer to the famous puzzler might be.[16]

[16] For a glimpse of the history and problems of this question see Küng. For the importance of the problem in modern Catholic theology see: von Balthasar, ad loc. For the history in greater detail see: Spindeler, *Cur Verbum caro Factum?* (for the 4th and 5th centuries, one-sided);

"Would the Son of God have become man if man had not sinned?" Put this way the question is academic and an invitation to the most sterile sort of speculation. But the issues involved are by no means unreal, nor need an attempt to deal with these issues be speculative. Let us reword the question to avoid the supposition contrary to fact: "Did God decree that the Incarnation should take place in view of foreseen and permitted sin, or did He allow sin in view of the unconditionally decreed Incarnation?" Did God decide that Jesus Christ should come in view of some third factor? Is an "in view of" involved here at all?

All possible exterior motives for the Incarnation are included in what takes place because of God's negative will. God says "Yes," and "No" in order to say "Yes." This we already know. Now we ask: Is this "No" in any way an independent factor? Barth denies that it is. And this too we could have guessed. But we must still ask: *Why* is a "No" necessary to the "Yes"? In view of some other factor? The foreseen interruption of sin?[17] Or simply in order that the "Yes" be the particular "Yes" which God in fact chooses to speak?

Obviously, Barth can operate for long stretches on a level where God's judgment and condemnation is simply His reaction to human sin and where the Incarnation is decreed in view of

---

Bissen, *La tradition sur la predestination absolue de Jesus-Christ du VIIIe au XIIIe siècle;* Dorner, *Christologie,* ad loc.; Hirsch, *Geschichte der neueren evangelischen Theologie,* vol. V, pp. 379–86; Féret, *Creati in Christo Jesu.*

[17] This would appear to be the view of Hans Küng (pp. 163, 165, 168). Küng believes himself in full agreement with Barth in this area. Insofar as he does not seem to appreciate how radical Barth's "supralapsarianism" is and is himself a Thomist on this precise point, he is mistaken in this belief. For both Barth and Küng, God's decision to send his Son is at once the eternal origin of all things and an answer to sin. But Barth goes on to a level of reflection where the decree to save from sin is not conditioned by the existence of sin. It does not seem to me that Küng does this.

the factually existing problems of human life. But it is typical of his theology that he again and again becomes involved in the problem of the dialectical position of this whole level of thought. It is typical that he repeatedly becomes involved in the question of the absoluteness of the Incarnation.

His most exact discussion of the matter appears as a long excursus on the conflict between infralapsarianism and supralapsarianism within orthodox Calvinist theology. (Barth's discussion is one of the best introductions to what often appears an impenetrable thicket of gratuitous language.) Barth describes the two schools as follows.

The supralapsarians taught that God from the beginning chose to show His mercy and His greatness through the salvation of certain individual men and the damnation of others. In order to be able to do this, He decreed the creation of the world and permitted the fall into sin. To be sure, all Calvinists spoke of an eternal decree of God embracing these three elements. But the peculiarly supralapsarian doctrine was the "in order that," the precise statement of the connection between the elements of God's decree. In order that man be saved or condemned—and so God's glory shown—man had to be a sinner, and in order to be a sinner he had to exist. Therefore God chose man to salvation or damnation prior to his creation and fall. (II/2, 136–9; 127–9)

The infralapsarians did not feel they had such exact information about the course of God's deliberations; they were unwilling to specify the connection between the elements of God's will so neatly. So they spoke of two decrees of God: First, His decision to create the world and allow the fall and second, His decree of predestination, which they understood exactly as did the supralapsarians. What they would not do was unite the two by making the decree of predestination the motive for the decision to create man and allow sin. They believed that God's motives in making this second decision were unknowable or at best only very generally knowable. To be sure, the two decrees are unfathomably one—but unfathomably. The one does not explain the other.

As a result of this split, the decree of creation and permission becomes in the infralapsarian view a given presupposition of the decree of predestination. God's decision to show mercy and power is not the absolute beginning of all things; it is the beginning of God's ways with man as he, within God's other decree, in fact stands there—created and fallen. (II/2, 139f.; 129f.)

Note that the difference between the two positions is simply definable: In the infralapsarian view God's decision to show mercy and power, to stand in covenant with man, is made in view of a third factor, the otherwise decided creation and fall of man.[18] The supralapsarians wanted to exclude any such relativizing of God's work of grace and judgment.

Both parties operated within certain presuppositions which Barth rejects: The object of predestination is the individual man as such. God chooses some to salvation and some to damnation, and these two works stand in stable coordination. The decision itself is the "absolute decree" of a distant and awful "highest being." As we will see in the chapter on predestination all of these motifs are abhorrent to Barth.

If we must choose between the two, Barth sees something to be said for both sides. But if we eliminate the false presuppositions then the supralapsarians have the decided advantage. And the advantage that Barth sees is precisely the "in order that," the absolute position of God's will to be righteous and merciful, the elimination of that indefinite and unrevealed will of God which

[18] One could also point to the separation between creation and reconciliation as the meaning of the infralapsarian position.

according to the infralapsarians is behind creation and fall, the elimination of the contingency of God's covenant-will, the elimination of the "in view of." (II/2, 143–7; 133–6)

Barth then makes the experiment of reconstructing the supralapsarian doctrine on other presuppositions. (II/2, 151–3; 140–2) If we see that the object of predestination is primarily Jesus Christ, that the goal of God's work is not mercy and justice in separation but a just mercy, and that the God who predestines is the Father of Jesus Christ, we arrive at the following: At the beginning God has chosen to share and reveal Himself and His glory. This means He has willed man, willed that there should be someone to share and apprehend His glory. He has not willed man in the abstract; "humanity" can not enter a real fellowship. He has willed *a* man, His chosen man. He has willed him as the witness of His glory and so as the object of His love. He is to confirm and reveal God's will by reflecting it back to Him in all its richness; He is to repeat God's eternal decision in the manifold decisions of created life.

The eternal decision of God is a double one. God is God and is not not-God; He eternally discriminates himself from what He is not, what He wills from what He does not will. He has chosen fellowship and rejected separation, chosen the world He did create and rejected the chaos which might have been. In this eternal self-discrimination God has His life and His glory; it is of this that the chosen man is to be a witness. And so the chosen man's repetition of God's will must also be double. He is to be witness of God's "Yes" and of God's "No." He is to choose what God has chosen and reject what God has rejected. And thus he is to live in complete covenant with God.

This means that the chosen man must be confronted with that

which God has rejected, as God confronted himself with it. But, since he is man and not God, he is thus confronted with a power superior to himself. His conquest and rejection of evil can not "be so self-evident as it was in God's case." (II/2, 152; 141) It can only occur as the content of a succession of events, in the course of the history of a deficiency and its remedy, of judgment and acquittal, of defeat and victory. What in God himself is the simple and immediate triumph of light over darkness must, in the created sphere, have the form of a history. It must, in time, be a *progression.* (II/2, 152; 141) "God does not will . . . evil and the fall and an act of sin on the part of this man . . . but for the sake of the fullness of his glory, . . . for the sake of the perfection of his love, He wills . . . this man as sinful man, i.e., as man ladened with sins. . . ." (II/2, 152; 141)

In that God wills the chosen man He wills this path. He wills man as the one who since he is not God is not equal to the threat and so wills himself as this man's helper. He wills to be the one through whose grace alone man shall live and so wills man as the one who is entirely dependent upon grace.

He wills that man shall be the one who *has been* freed by God from the rule of sin, who *has been* rescued from death. God wills that man shall be fallible man, not because He wants him to fall but because He wills that as the fallen man he should be witness of God's complete glory, of His "Yes" *and* His "No." He wills fallible man, not that he fall but that he be lifted from the fall by God's power. (II/2, 153; 141f.) The reader is invited to ponder this last sentence; it is the key to Barth's whole theological structure.

We already have the answer to the question of this section. But certain difficulties remain. How can God will the existence of the fallen sinner without willing his fall? What can be meant by the man who does not sin but is nevertheless a sinner? To see our way through we must ask: *Who* is this chosen man?

He is Jesus Christ. But how can it be said of Him that He was freed from the rule of sin and rescued from the fall? We must go on to say, Jesus Christ not in isolation but in His work of rescuing all other men. For He does not exist in isolation; His life is His work for others.

Of *this* chosen man it can well be said that He was sinful without sinning, rescued from the fall without falling. Again, who is this chosen one? "This man, who as God's Son is the King of His people, is elected man." (II/2, 62; 58) The chosen man is Jesus Christ, with and for the others who are not Jesus Christ but belong to Him. We begin to see how He can be saved from a fall which is not His, but is still a real fall.

To probe deeper, we ask: To what was this chosen man chosen? Barth answers: He was chosen from all eternity to die. In that God chooses Him, He also rejects and condemns Him. For the choice of Jesus Christ necessarily includes the rejection of what is not chosen and its existence as the object of that rejection. Now Jesus Christ is a creature. But the creature *as such*, just because it is only a creature, is helpless against what God rejects. It must sin, and so God's eternal choice of the creature Jesus Christ is the condemnation of the creature as such. But it is precisely this man-as-such, this creature-in-himself, whom God has from eternity chosen for fellowship with Himself—*in* that one chosen man for whom the possibility of sin does *not* exist. Therefore Jesus' choice means that He must bear the rejection of the man-as-such who is chosen in Him, that He must defend the lost creature against the onslaught of evil. God's election of Christ is thus in and of itself, in its own inner necessity, an election of the rejected. Jesus is chosen to die. (II/2, 130–3; 122–5)

Thus there comes into view that creature-as-such who can and must fall, who dares not withstand the attack of evil in his own power because his destiny is to withstand it by God's covenant grace. Yet he is not immediately a partaker of this grace but is destined to *become* such. (III/3, 410; 355f.) He does not come into view as a reality existing independently of God's decision that Christ shall exist. Rather he comes into view in the very course of our search for the inner structure of that decision.

Once again, who is the chosen man? We remember: In that God chooses this man He chooses a history, a progress. This follows immediately from the foregoing; Jesus Christ is His history with His people. What is this history? It is the history of a judgment and acquittal, of defeat and victory. It is the history in which man is rejected and chosen, denied and affirmed, in which he lives *in the passage* from the one to the other. (IV/1, 575f.; 516f.) This history is the imitation within human time of the eternal decision of God.

Here we must digress for a moment. According to Barth, God is not timeless but rather the Lord of time. The time which He has in His eternal aliveness is the possibility and model of created time. But there is this fundamental difference between God's time and created time: In God past, present, and future are not separated. In merely creaturely time they fall apart into a succession of separate "times." In God the past is present as the eternally past, as the, so to speak, qualitatively past. For man the past is that which is no more.

And so with God that which He rejects is *always* past, qualitatively past. But when this rejection is repeated in man's time, this past acquires a time of its own. The triumph of light over darkness is for God an ever-present immediate event. In human time it becomes a succession of events—with a "before" when this triumph has not yet happened. In human time there was a time when the sin and evil rejected by God were present reality. Within the whole history of Jesus Christ and His people, *our* time, all the time we spend by ourselves, is exactly this time. (I/2, 50ff.; 45ff.) Thus the creature-in-itself and the evil bondage to which it is inevitably fallen acquire a time of their own. God wills Jesus Christ and His history. The sinful creature is that *from* which this history moves. God wills the chosen man's history in time with those who are not in themselves the chosen man. Now we can finally understand how this chosen one, who does not fall, is nevertheless raised from the fall.

God wills the elevation of man. He wills evil and His own struggle against it only for the sake of this elevation. He wills the way to this goal. (II/2, 190ff.; 173ff.)

Again man-as-such, the man who must fall, has appeared—now not only as a possibility but as the possessor of a time of his own, as an historical reality. The reality of sin has appeared, not independently, but as we have penetrated into the nature of Jesus' election.[19]

It is time to state the conclusion of this section. According to Barth, sin is not, either as accident or as permitted by God, a third factor which motivates God to decide on that order of reconciliation which He has in fact chosen. Election involves judgment, God's "Yes" and His "No," solely in order to be the

[19] It is worth stating at this point that all that was said at the end of the section on *Nihility* remains in full force. Barth does *not* teach that sin is necessary or even possible. It has no inner consistency nor does it have a basis in creation or grace. How Barth maintains both sides of this dialectic may be puzzling, but I think I have made the distinctions he draws reasonably clear. Whether or not they are convincing the reader must judge for himself—from a perusal of Barth's own text.

particular kind of election, the particular "Yes," which God in fact chooses to speak. This "Yes" is Jesus Christ; the decision of God that He should exist exactly as He did and does exist, is absolute. Whatever else happens, happens solely in order that this work of God's right hand be the particular work which God has chosen to do. There is no other factor.[20]

[20] Have we gone too fast? Are we sure that Barth sees no third factor in view of which God decreed salvation? An attentive reader may very well have two further possibilities in mind:

At several points we have heard Barth speak in terms which might presuppose an immanent problem of extra-divine existence as such, so that if God decided to move outside Himself at all He would *then* be forced to do so in the way we have described. It cannot be said that Barth is entirely clear here. But a moment's reflection will convince us that this cannot be Barth's intention. He, of all people, cannot picture God as first deciding to create and then having to take counsel as to how this might be carried out in view of conditions "out there." "God does not stand under any alien law, any general truth and possibility and presupposition embracing and conditioning and limiting both Himself and the world and man." (IV/1, 590; 529) The problem of extra-divine existence which Barth postulates must be one which is not independent of God but one of which He is Himself the author. The realm outside of God arises in the first place only because of His election of grace. Such necessities as may rule there must have been set by God's free decision as He has made it. And the problem in virtue of which nihility arises and is more powerful than the creature cannot therefore be set by an independent law of extra-divine existence. It must be the result of God's *opus alienum,* of the permission which accompanies His positive will because it is the particular will which it is.

Finally, it might be said that God himself is a given factor in view of which His will for man, if He chooses to have one, must be that will which it is. Everything goes back to His eternal act of self-discrimination, to the eternal act in which He is God and not-God. May it not be that the eternal nature of God thus posited constitutes a given condition, in view of which everything must go as we have seen if God then turns outside Himself? Not so, according to Barth. This act of choice and the decree of election are factually the same act; although God could have been God in some other act than in election *ad extra,* it is, in fact, in this act that He is God. God's essence does not constitute a given condition for him.

But this question does lead us to the final step in understanding just how radically Barth understands the absoluteness of the Incarnation. We have an explicit statement on the motive of the Incarnation: "For what reason . . .? Because He willed to have mercy on this creature, and did have mercy. . . . Why . . .? Because He is the God of this mercy. . . .There is no sense in trying to find . . . any other reason for the fact that the Word became

It is in order that grace really be grace that God also rejects, that He also performs an *opus alienum*. "It is the very essence of our reconciliation as grace, to depend on the existence of a divine *voluntas permittens,* and in virtue of this on the reality of disgrace, damnation and hell." (II/1, 672; 595) The Incarnation is its own sole reason. The existence of Jesus Christ *is* the will of God and: "The will of God knows no Wherefore? It is an absolute Therefore, the ultimate Therefore of all." (II/2, 20; 20)

---

flesh. . . ." (IV/2, 45f.; 43) For it is indeed true that the eternal election of grace is at once the basis of all relations between God *and* the act in which God is God. Therefore Barth can go so far as to say—of course within the freedom in which God is what He is—that *it is essential to God to be incarnate in sinful flesh.* (II/1, 581; 517) The absoluteness of the Incarnation is the absoluteness of God.

CHAPTER THREE

CHRIST THE ALPHA

We have already talked of God "doing" this and that "in eternity." This sort of talk has undoubtedly given distress to some readers. But at this point I will ask them to contain themselves yet a while. For the present we will assume that eternity is a realm in which things may be done and ask what sort of event Barth asserts takes place there.

In the previous chapter we have seen that according to Barth the history of salvation and all history is the implementation of an eternal decree of God. "In eternity" God "made a decree," "decided," "predestined," "formed a plan." We have used several such expressions for this event. We now ask: What sort of event is this? What kind of reality pertains to it? This decision of God controls our temporal history. What is the manner of this control?

If again we answer immediately we will perhaps produce something like this: In eternity God conceived a plan. Since then He has been engaged, step by step, in giving reality to this plan. And if we have been instructed by the previous chapter we may remark that it was an odd sort of plan, that God seems, like Hegel's absolute, to have a passion for the long way around. We may wonder at God, who seems to have deliberately created man in an untenable position and to have taken a generous amount of time about coming to help him.

In so answering we will once again encounter Barth's protest. When *God* "decides," when *He* "forms a plan," this act has quite a different sort of reality than that presupposed by our answer. The task of this chapter will be to show how Barth reverses the usual order of "plan" and "execution" at every step, to display his doctrine of the supreme reality of God's eternal history.

The Preexistence of Jesus Christ

I

Before all time God chose to relate himself to a reality other than himself and chose what that relation would be. What He chose was that He would unite Himself, in the person of Jesus Christ, with a rebellious creature; He chose to be God as one person with the man Jesus. (II/2, 107f.; 99ff.) Here we come to a major assertion of Barth's theology, one that makes us stop. Barth asserts that the event of this choice is the event of the preexistence of Jesus Christ. He asserts that Jesus' life, the life of the God-*man,* happened eternally in that God made this choice. He *was* God's covenant decree, and therefore He existed in eternity before all time. His existence is identical with the act of God's choosing. (II/2, 109; 101f.)

In eternity it was decreed that Jesus Christ should live; in eternity He already existed. Both assertions are made by Barth; he holds that they are equivalent. In eternity God chose *to be* Jesus Christ and in the act of choosing *was* Jesus Christ.

How can we understand this? God chose to be bound to man. As an act of choice this act was a self-determination on God's part. Therefore the act of choice was itself already the chosen state of affairs, since what was chosen was exactly this determination of God's life. Or again: God chose to be Jesus Christ.

But who is Jesus Christ? He is the reality of God's unity with man. Now since in making this choice God committed himself to man, since in making this choice God united His fate with man's fate, we can say that the act of choice is already the existence of Jesus Christ. Or again: In making this choice God concludes a covenant with man, He closes an agreement with him. But the existence of this covenant and the existence of Jesus Christ are the same thing.

And so Jesus Christ is not only the one who is chosen by God, as we saw in the last chapter. He is also the God who does the choosing. "Jesus Christ is the electing God." (II/2, 110f.; 103f.) The "God" of whom we spoke all through the last chapter as choosing this and deciding that has been identified. He is not a highest being-in-general. He is not the hidden arbiter of classical Calvinism. He is the One who walked, slept, and worked in Palestine, was crucified under Pontius Pilate, and now lives as Lord of the Church.

"Jesus Christ is the electing God." More precisely, the Son *in* His eternally chosen unity with the Son of man is the God who choses. (II/2, 111; 103f.) But this does not mean only as the Son who *planned* to become one with man. Jesus Christ, the God-man, not just the eternal Son as such, is the one who in all eternity decides on grace. (II/2, 112f.; 104ff.) Barth argues that between the eternal being of the Second Person of the Trinity and the temporal existence of the man Jesus there is a "third" reality—the reality of the choice in which the Son chooses to be *and is* one with man. (II/2, 114ff.; 106ff.) The God whose decision rules all history is the preexistent God-man Jesus Christ.

Let us be clear about this. Barth is not being rhetorical. He means that Jesus the Christ, the Son of God as man, was eternally preexistent. He means that in a particular but very real sense the Incarnation *happened* in eternity before all time. (II/2, 157, 172, IV/1, 70; 145, 158, 66) To understand this act of choice which is the origin of all that happens outside God we must look

> upwards to the place where the incarnation, the reality of the divine-human person of Jesus Christ, before the foundation of the world and all other reality, is identical with the eternal purpose . . . of God, and where the eternal purpose of the good-pleasure of God which precedes all created reality is identical with the reality of the divine-human person of Jesus Christ . . . upwards to the place where the eternal God not only foresees and foreordains this person, but where He Himself . . . actually is this person. (II/2, 116; 108)

Barth calls this a "third" level of reality. On the one hand there is the existence of the Son in and of Himself, who could have chosen to be and have been other than one person with the man Jesus. On the other hand there is the chosen human nature considered in isolation. Between them there is the *self-determination* of the Son in which He is one with humanity and so as God-man the subject even of the act of determination (II/2, 114f.; 106–8) Between the pure being of the triune God and the temporal history of salvation this "third" reality is the concrete decree of grace, a decision which falls in the inner life of the triune God, the "Word" who is identical with Jesus. (II/2, 117f.; 109f.)

II

We will get no further with this matter until we know something of Barth's doctrine of God. Spending a few paragraphs on this will be no hardship, for the volume which treats it is one of the most splendidly developed in the *Church Dogmatics,* and one of the most useful.[1] It is the opening discussion of God as the one who "loves in freedom" which we will consider.

Barth asserts that all Christian theology must stem from absolute confidence in the veracity of God's self-revelation in Christ. Its first proposition is therefore that God is in himself no different than He is in His revelation. But in the life and works of Jesus Christ we have to do, not with a static "being," but with an event, with happenings. God has not revealed himself through formulas or through oracles or through images but through a life history. It follows that God's being is also an event, a *deed,* and not the static peace of pure "isness" which theologians have often described. God's activity, His doing, is ultimate, is not transcended by a static "being." God *is* event, act, life. He is the Living One. Barth borrows a scholastic formula, gives it a characteristic superlative and calls God *actus purissimus,* "perfectly pure event." [2] (II/1, 294–6; 262–4)

But God's revelation is a particular event, not "event" in general. It is the event of Jesus' life. Therefore we must add a word to the definition: God is *actus purus particularis,* "a particular pure event." God as event is unique in that He is the source and origin of all events, the event of events. But He is also unique in the much simpler, but at present more important, sense that He is this event and not that event, that He is one individual event.

The individuality of the Event which is God is its freedom. God is in Himself a free event. This freedom is that of a *person.*[3]

[1] Though it is also one of the worst translated.

[2] Of course "act" bears a different meaning than in the scholastic usage—though Barth's use is in some respects not so far from that of *Thomas.*

[3] Barth also uses the word "spirit," in the sense which it derives from the German philosophical tradition.

God is always "I," never "It." He is never even "He" or "Him." (II/1, 296–300; 264–8)

God is *always* "I," never "It" or "He." This is the difference between Him and other "persons"; this is the unique freedom which is His individuality. For we, as created and derived persons, are sometimes "it," sometimes less than free and creative subjects of our own acts, sometimes mere links in chains of compulsion. And we are surely often "he," subjects to be sure, but not at the moment the subjects who are doing the acting and deciding and creating. But God is the person whose personhood knows no infringements, not those coming from other persons and things, and not even those arising out of Himself. This brings us to the final mark of the specific freedom of God's acting. He is the "I" who disposes of His own nature, who posits and marks off His own self. My freedom as an "I," as a deciding and creating subject, is limited by the nature which I simply have and over which my control is limited. For example, I am so constituted that I can only remember, not relive, the past; I am so made and that ends the matter. God's personhood is not so limited. *He himself decides what He shall be, what His nature shall be.* He is therefore the one and only perfectly authentic "I." (II/1, 296–304; 265–272)

All this means finally that God's being is His decision! He is that act which is not based on anything prior to itself; only decision in pure form is such an act. He is the authentic "I"; only in deciding does one dispose of one's own characteristics. *God is His own decision.*[4] (II/1, 305; 271f.)

[4] In the section on "God's Being in Freedom" Barth looks longer at this unique freedom of God. There are two sides to it: His independence from other beings, the freedom of His *opera ad extra,* is the side we first think of. But more fundamental is His freedom in Himself. He is free to begin with Himself, to exist only by virtue of His own existence, to exist without presup-

We return to our more immediate subject. God is His own decision. Very well, what has He decided? What decision is it that is His Being? It is precisely the same decision we have spoken of all through the study. It is that same decision which is, according to Barth, the preexistence of Jesus Christ. We may now go on with our attempt to pin down the "third" reality which is the reality of Jesus' preexistence.

This third reality is an event in the life of the triune God, an event in which He decides what He is, an event which *is* His Being—so that we may well speak of God the Son being eternally the God-man. The difference between this reality and the Being of the eternal Son *as such* lies solely in the fact that this eternal identity of the Son and Jesus is a choice—the Son *could have* existed otherwise without being any more or less the Son. But He has not. Jesus preexists as an event of choice which is the eternal Being of God.

But surely Barth is going completely wild! It is of course no novelty but the basic foundation of all Christian theology that

---

positions. Barth asserts that God does not even need His own Being in order to be who He is. By this he intends to prevent the misunderstanding that the fact that God exists by virtue only of His existence means that His existence is accidental, that He could "not-be," in Barth's language, that He "needs" His Being to be, that He has to *establish* His own Being. Rather the act of God's existence is not the production of His being but the confirmation of the Being which He always has. This act of existence is free even from the possibility of nonexistence; it suffers under no necessity, not even that of establishing its own being. Yet only with caution is God to be called *ens necessarium*. For that the act of God's Being always has Being, does not produce but confirms Being, is only true in the *decision* which this act is. That God cannot "not-be" is His own factual decision. God did not have to be; even here He stands under no necessity.

From here we come to God's negative freedom, His independence of all other reality. When the matter is taken in this order it is clear that the existence of other beings can constitute no problem for God, since His freedom is not grounded in His relationship to other reality but in Himself. (II/1, 334ff.; 297ff.)

Jesus Christ and God are one. But by regarding this unity as a fact of God's eternal and changeless being, by teaching a pre-existence of the God-*man* in the pretemporal eternity of the Trinity, is not Barth branching off into gnostic mythology? [5]

Not necessarily. For Barth—and this is no peculiarity of his—teaches that the existence of Jesus Christ as the God-man is the point where eternity is time, is the point of union between them. (II/1, 694ff.; 615ff.) Thus the presence in eternity of the God-man is not mythological; it is the human history of Jesus Christ, His birth, death, and proclaimed resurrection, which is "in" eternity, without needing to leave its human time and place under Pontius Pilate in Palestine. For this is an event which is at once an event in God and an event in God's work in time; it is the passage from the one to the other, or better yet, the event of their unification. (II/2, 2–6; 2–6)

At this point one may breathe a sigh of relief—and fall victim to a misunderstanding. We may conclude that Barth means nothing more drastic than that the event of Christ's life is "eternally valid" or some such thing.[6] Or we may conclude that Barth means that Jesus Christ, since He is also the eternal Son, is indirectly eternal.

This would be an error. It is true that the event of Jesus' existence is an event in which eternity and time fall together. But it is just this event which *establishes* this unity, and within this unity God's eternity retains its priority. Jesus' existence is first an eternal event *and then,* by virtue of the unity of time and eternity created within itself, an event in created time. The

[5] See note 16 on this chapter.

[6] Barth has this side of the matter too. See III/2, 525ff.; 437ff. But here we deal with the Son as the man Jesus, not with the man Jesus as the Son.

distinction between eternity and time is not to be blurred.[7] (II/2, 107, 111, 203; 99f., 103f., 185)

The preexistence of Jesus Christ the God man must be described with a "before." (II/1, 701; 621f.) Before Bethlehem, before creation, in God's pure eternity before He turned to time, Jesus Christ the God-man happened.

And finally, though it cause us consternation, we must be clear that Barth is not thinking of the kind of existence which all things have before their creation, in the plan and intention of the Creator. He specifically denies it. (II/2, 110f.; 104) God is indeed eternally present to all creatures. But although they and their time are enclosed in God's eternal time, they are in their time and not in His. (II/1, 692–4; 614) Jesus Christ is in God's time.

His preexistence is rather at the other end of the scale. It takes place in God's "eternal self-differentiation from all that is

[7] Nor is the eternal preexistence of the God-man exhausted in His immediacy to God's all-encompassing eternity. To be sure, God's eternity as existence before all time does not exclude but includes time and history. (I/1, 447f.; 487f.) God's eternity is not only pretemporal, it is also supertemporal and posttemporal. (II/1, 700ff.; 621ff.) In its supertemporality eternity accompanies and bears time, is immediately present to all times. (II/1, 702–9; 623–9) Thus it is that God's act of election, made before all time, is nevertheless not a fixed system, determining all things from the past, but God's *life*. As pretemporal it is also supertemporal and posttemporal. It accompanies time; it has occurred, but it also occurs and will occur. Thus it is always immediate; God *lives* as the God who chooses. (II/2, 201; 183) Nevertheless eternity is not time, nor are the three "times" of eternity the same. It makes a difference with which aspect of His eternity an event is connected. (II/1, 720ff.; 638 ff.) Election is pretemporal, and only as such also supertemporal and posttemporal. (II/2, 201; 183) It occurred in the time before time, in the time when it was decreed that there should *be* time and its content. It *was* this decree. Before time, in the pure eternity of God, other reality and God's involvement therewith was decreed, God turned outside of himself, the Son was determined as *incarnandum*. (II/1, 701; 622) "For Jesus Christ is before all time, and therefore eternally the Son . . ., God Himself in His turning to the world . . ., to a time distinct from His eternity. . . ." (II/1, 701; 622).

not God and is not willed by God." (II/2, 152; 141) It takes place in the act in which God is God. (II/2, 54–8; 51–5) It is "the living act in which He affirms and posits Himself and everything that is. . . ." (II/1, 661f.; 587) It is an eternal event in God himself. (II/2, 82; 76f.) The act of election, which is the event of the God-man's preexistence, is an event in the eternal trinitarian life of God.[8]

Eternal History

The last sentence above leads directly to the question: In what sense does God have a history? We are accustomed to think of God in terms of abstract timelessness; the habit of describing Him in terms of "pure," and so static, characteristics such as "pure justice," "pure love," and so forth is so built into us as to be nearly unconscious. An "advanced" conception of God is very likely to be one of "pure substance," visually pictured as an infinitely extended pudding (to steal someone's devastating remark). If we also believe in the Christian message about God's entry into history, we are almost certain to regard this entry as His emergence into a foreign and slightly distasteful realm and to regard His *doing* anything as an act of condescension.

Barth takes the opposite view. God is in and of Himself an historical being. We are the ones who tend to be static.

I

What does Barth mean by "history"? He has given an explicit definition:

The history of a being begins, continues and is completed when

[8] To all this, see also IV/2, 372–401; 333–59.

something other than itself and transcending its own nature encounters it, approaches it and determines its being in the nature proper to it, so that it is compelled and enabled to transcend itself in response and in relation to this new factor. (III/2, 189; 158)

There are three notes in this definition. First, history is self-transcendence. History happens when I leave what I *am* and move out toward what I *am not* yet. Historical life is life which abandons the security of the present in a leap into the non-given, the presently nonexistent. Second, this movement of self-transcendence is possible only in confrontation with another. An isolated being is necessarily a static, ahistorical being. I cannot move out from myself unless there is an outside, a reality distinct from myself, to move to. I cannot move from what I am to what I am not unless there *is* a that-which-I-am-not. That is to say, history is only possible in communion between persons. For only another person finally resists my absorbing all things into myself; only a person is irreducibly an other. Finally, the horizon within which this meeting takes place is *time*. An essentially timeless being could not transcend itself, could not be what it is not. Only in time can I as the same person be both bachelor and husband, in that I the bachelor *become* I the husband. Only in time can persons meet and determine each other, for here again a before and after is essentially presupposed.[9]

From this definition of history we can understand how, for Barth, God is the eminently historical being. He is not timeless in the sense that He is bereft of time. He *has* time. His eternity is the very model and source of our time. In Him there is beginning, middle, and end, there is origin, movement, and goal.

[9] You will see that Barth's definition of history is one typical of modern thought. In my own explication of Barth's definition the echoes of Heidegger and Feuerbach are obvious.

But He rules them; we are ruled by them. For Him these do not fall apart but are possessed together in a *now* which is vastly more active, in which infinitely more is begun and carried along and finished, than in the before, now, and afterward of our created imitation. God has time; we are had by time. He is the eminently temporal being. Barth approves the definition of Boethius: *Aeternitas est interminabilis vitae tota simul et perfecta possessio.* "Eternity is the simultaneous and perfect possession of life without end." And he underlines the word "life." That God is eternal does not therefore mean that He is excluded from time; it means that He includes our time. His eternity is at once pre-, super-, and post-temporal; at all "times" we are enveloped in it. (II/1, 685–722; 608–40)

Nor is God solitary. He not only has, but *is* communion, quite apart from His communion with creatures. He is triune. The Father, Son, and Spirit *practice* the love and freedom which God is. He is the Living One, from eternity and of himself. I.e., God *is* in that He is *busy,* in that He is eternally active in His inner relationships as Father, Son, and Holy Spirit. He exists in that He wills and knows Himself, in that He loves, in that He makes use of His freedom. His whole being and action toward an exterior reality is but the overflow of His inner being and action. (II/2, 192; 175) God lives in personal communion and therefore has history. But unlike us He is not dependent for this communion upon other persons; as the one personal triune God He *is* interpersonal history. Therefore He is the eminently historical being.[10]

[10] It is worth noting and applauding the *substantive* use which Barth here makes of the doctrine of the Trinity. If the Christian answer to the question "Who is God?" is "He is the Triune God," then our description of Him should be affected by this.

And so God is the One who preeminently *becomes*. As the eternal He lives in our time. As the Creator He is one of His creatures. For He is the One who *is* His own decision.[11]

Therefore, God's being as the Triune is itself a history, the history of the Father, Son, and Holy Spirit among themselves. But more important for our considerations, all of His works outside Himself are but the overflow of this eternal animation of God, and therefore are also history. And, as the passage from the one history to the other, the eternal decision of God, which is identical with the preexistence of Jesus Christ, is necessarily preeminently event, act, and history. It is history in that it is the eternal presence before God of Jesus Christ. It is history as the meeting of God with man, with the man Jesus Christ. (II/2, 192; 175f.)

There is a confrontation and a decision between God and man in the eternal bosom of God. (II/2, 197; 180) In the person of Jesus Christ God and man meet in an eternal event and there occurs in God's eternal time the very origin and model of all other historical events. (II/2, 194; 177) There is an eternal history. (II/2, 202; 184) The preexistence of Jesus Christ the God-man is a preeminently historical event.

It is this same event which Barth means when he speaks of

[11] Barth has not formulated a general definition of "history," measured God against it, found Him adequate, and so defined Him as "historical." At least this is not Barth's intention. I am sure he would say that he has read his definition of history from our knowledge of God given in His revelation, that the real question is not whether God has a history but whether any other beings do.

Some doubt is thrown on the claim that this is the real order of Barth's thought by the remarkable resemblance of his conception of history to that of other modern thinkers who by no means suppose themselves to derive their definitions from revelation. But I would be prepared to argue that the contemporary concern for history and the contemporary understanding of its nature is a secularized version of an insight of faith.

the "original covenant" between God and man. (II/2, 171; 157) The eternal covenant is covenant history. And as the history of the *original* covenant, of the fundamental meeting and compact between God and man, it stands in a fundamental relation to all other history. Barth uses the term "primal history." [12] This history is the basis of all other history between God and man. (II/2, 7; 8f.) As a history in God, who is the origin of all things, it is the law of all other history. It is the interior secret, the hidden origin and goal, first of the temporal history of salvation and so of all history. (II/2, 202ff.; 184ff.) It is the "inner basis" of the covenant. (III/1, 106f.; 97) Barth finally reaches a very radical formulation: This history is the "principle and essence of all happening. . . ." (II/2, 201; 183)

The matter reaches its final formulation when Barth says of Jesus Christ, of the historical event of His existence, that He is the inner-divine principle and possibility of all relationship, of all fellowship, between God and His creatures. (II/1, 356f.; 317) It is He and His history that are "principle and essence of all happening. . . ."

II

The content of this eternal history is salvation. The meeting and compact between God and man, which is the preexistence of Jesus Christ, is salvation history, and that in the exact sense. The content of this history is point for point that of the history of the birth, life, death, and resurrection of Jesus of Nazareth. The eternal history is nothing other than the decisive factors of Jesus' history as events in eternity. To put the matter in extreme form: Everything that happened in Jesus Christ's history on

[12] *Urgeschichte.*

earth happened in eternity, and in God's pretemporal eternity at that.

According to Barth the being of Jesus Christ consists in two inseparable events: (1) the self-humiliation of the Son of God and (2) the elevation of the Son of man. God binds himself to sinful man and so binds sinful man to himself. In these two events the history which bears the name Jesus Christ is, so far as its essential content is concerned, exhausted.[13] Now precisely these same two sides constitute the act of choice which God made in eternity. (II/2, 171; 157) The concretion of God's will which occurs in eternity already means that God gives up His immunity to the onslaught of evil. Not only does the covenant in *time* mean that God must undergo the evil which comes with his sinful covenant partner; but also the *eternal* covenant is already a covenant with man the sinner and requires God's substitutionary involvement with evil. In His eternal act of choice God then and there opens himself to the attack of evil in order to be in covenant with man. Indeed, He then and there makes himself the object of His own condemnation. (II/2, 177ff.; 162ff.)

Therefore the once-for-all, the "It-is-finished," of God's self-sacrifice for man's salvation is not, according to Barth, limited to the events in Palestine. He can use exactly the same expressions about salvation as that which happened in eternity before all time—once for all. Of God's self-humiliation he says:

God's election as the beginning of all things is God's self-surrender in his eternal decree. His self-surrender: for God gave—and this is not something that has just now happened, it is eternal divine *fore*ordination—his own Son, He spoke his Word. And therewith He surrendered himself, He gave himself up . . . for the good . . .

[13] See below, pp. 123ff.

of the man whom He created and who had fallen away from him. (II/2, 176; 161)[14]

Of the creature's resultant unity with God he says: "He has taken the creature to himself even before it was, namely, in His own Son, who willed to live and die as a man for all men, as a creature for all creatures. He thus took it to Himself even in its very contradiction." (III/1, 436; 380f.) Man is "the one whom God loved from all eternity in His Son . . . the one to whom He gave Himself from all eternity in His Son. . . ." (II/2, 180; 165)

We can come to the same point from the anthropological viewpoint. These two sides of salvation history are, considered as things that God does *to man,* man's justification and his sanctification. Barth regards both of these as already realized in the pretemporal eternity of God's decree: God can declare us sinners to be righteous and speak the truth because *the* truth, the Word in which all things are made and in which the true nature of all things is decided, was from eternity God's "No" to sin and his "Nevertheless yes" to the sinner. From all eternity God has set his Word victoriously against the whole world of evil and against the sin of each individual man—as the "Nevertheless" of forgiveness. He has never apprehended or known us otherwise than in his eternal Word, who is named Jesus Christ. (II/2, 850; 760)

Our sanctification, which is so notoriously hard to discover when we look into ourselves, is nevertheless real, *the* reality of our life. For the sanctified man exists and is named Jesus Christ. And since He is the Word which was in the beginning, since His life is the principle of all else that happens, His holiness is

[14] See note 14 to Chapter 2.

the very origin of our lives. Holiness is not something which has first to become real in our temporal existence. It is the truth about us before anything at all happens in our "own" lives. Our sanctification is so hard to discover in ourselves for the very reason that it is the superior reality *within* which we live from all eternity. (II/2, 870ff.; 777ff.)

And so the complex of relationships between God and man, the whole "kingdom of God," is eternally actual. The relation between God and man is originally that between God and man in the person of Jesus Christ. He, and so also our relation to God, was with God in the beginning as the beginning of all God's works. (II/2, 172f.; 158f.) In eternity God calls to man for faith and man answers. In eternity God creates a partner for himself and grants him a life of royal freedom. For this is what happens between God and man in Christ; He is the realized kingdom of God. (II/2, 194–8; 177–81)

Nor is this "kingdom," this animated relation between God and man, a relation in general, a neutral presupposition of the concrete history of God and sinful man. It is exactly that relation which is at Calvary, the action and reaction of forgiveness and gratitude or ingratitude. It is the kingdom of the King who gives himself for His subjects. The eternal will of God was the man "who is the wholehearted witness of God's Kingdom and enjoys as such a kingly freedom. . . ." And this man is not the postulated witness of a kingdom which might have been but "the Lamb of God which taketh away the sin of the world. . . ." It is this witness of this kingdom who is eternally willed by God. And that means that "This is the man who was in the beginning with God." *This* kingdom in the person of *this* witness is "not merely a temporal event." God is "the living God Himself in the beginning of all His ways" in that this history "between God and man" happens "in the bosom of God. . . ." (II/2, 197; 179f.)

To summarize this section: We have understood what happened in God's eternal act of choice only when we have seen that the whole complex history between God and man is real therein. The whole affair of God's call and man's answer happens in the eternal existence of Jesus Christ, in the divine act of will which is the eternal presupposition of all God's works. (II/2, 198; 180f.)

The destiny to salvation in which man is from eternity enclosed is therefore not an abstract plan but the reality of salvation itself. The decision about man has already been made. It is always behind us. It is the *terminus a quo* of human life. Even as a fallen sinner, man remains the one for whom God *has* from all eternity sacrificed His Son, whose rejection God *has* from all eternity taken upon himself. Man the sinner is not only destined for blessedness from all eternity, but the event in which he becomes and is blessed precedes his temporal existence. (II/2, 180–5; 165–9)

We come again to the concept of the eternal covenant which God made with himself about man in His pretemporal eternity. (II/2, 111; 104) As the beginning of all God's ways it creates a human life-situation which is "the situation of every single man." (II/2, 715; 643) The entire history of sin and repentance (or its failure) takes place inside the covenant of grace. Man, as he really is, is "a sinner, but . . . as such and in spite of himself . . . also the object of divine grace, the partner of the covenant. . . ." (III/2, 36; 32) It is only by virtue of his position as covenant partner with God that he can be a sinner. (III/2, 36; 32)

In sum, the entire reality of what has been called "the way of salvation" stands in force from all eternity. It is the superior reality within which the whole temporal drama is played. In that he goes his way on earth the creature will always find himself "in a very definite sense on God's way." (III/3, 106; 94)

III

At two points caution is indicated. First, Barth does not mean that the relation between God and man is a general state of affairs, so that instead of a real history between God and His individual covenant partners there would only be cases of a general truth. God's relation to man is always His concrete action in the lives of individual men. The covenant is not an idea but a history between God and a plurality of men. (III/2, 631f.; 523f.) Barth can and must say this because the pretemporal eternity in which the covenant precedes all our actions is also his super- and post-temporal eternity. God's eternal action is His life. And He has not ceased to be the living God; He has not retreated behind the letter of His decree. (II/2, 207f.; 188f.) But this does not change the fact that in all this we are concerned with God's eternity *before* time, which *as such* accompanies time. God has chosen. This means that Jesus Christ and all that is involved in His existence was with God before all time.

Second, we must remember that in speaking about what happened in eternity we are speaking of events in the modus of *pre*-destination. They are real in eternity *as* God's eternal will that they be real in time. It will not do to think of a sort of second world, very like this one, in which everything that happens here has an eternal double. It is God's *decision* that happens in eternity. But we have seen that God's eternal decision is very different from man's forming a plan. When we plan, our plan must then, as a second step, be given such reality as it is to have outside of our minds. With God it is different. God's decision is the eternal event of that which is decided. It is not a mere intention to do something but a real occurrence, the most real of all historical events.

Let us put the matter so: The full reality of what is recounted by Scripture as the history of salvation is brought into force by God in the event of His eternal decision and stands in force from that point on.

Eternal History and Jesus of Nazareth

Our next problem is in many ways the most difficult of this chapter. What is the relation between "eternal history" and the history of salvation as it runs in our time and space? What is the relation between Jesus Christ's preexistence and His life in our time? In putting this question, we do not suppose that Barth thinks of two different persons with two different histories. From the first, Barth has described this as the event in which God took time from our time to be His eternity, which is as one event an event in time and an event in eternity. (III/2, 569ff.; 474ff.) But we must still ask what the precise nature of this identity is.

For the most part Barth is content to describe the relation with an "and." God has acted on our behalf from eternity *and then* in the center of temporal history. (II/2, 702; 632) Accordingly he can speak quite simply of the reconciliation which happened in our time as the temporal realization of the eternal plan. (II/2, 819; 733) God decided in eternity what He would do and then in time He did it. (II/2, 508; 458) But the discussion in the last section makes it clear that this "and" conceals a highly dialectical relation. What we have just said only sharpens the problem. God has acted in eternity "and" in time. Very well—but it is just the meaning of this "and" that we want to discover.

I

Where Barth is more explicit he defines the relation in this way: What God does in the history of Jesus Christ on earth is the *implementation* and *revelation* of the eternal act of choice. (IV/2, 33f.; 31ff.) Of these two terms the second determines the meaning of the first. For all that is left to "implement" man's salvation is that it be made known. Jesus is the cause and means of our salvation *in that* He is its revealer. (II/2, 124–7; 116–8) Thus Barth can, if he chooses, continue the discussion of Jesus' human life and use the single term "revelation" as an equivalent for the double term. (IV/2, 36ff.; 34ff.)

God has chosen the man Jesus from all eternity. What has He chosen Him *for?* To be the *revelation* and *mirror* of God's decision of mercy (II/2, 124ff.; 116ff.), ". . . for the proclamation to many. . . ." (II/2, 492; 444) Perhaps the most striking passage in this connection is the following:

. . . if the saving work of Jesus consists in His laying down his life for his friends, this is the same thing, only in its aspect as a self-revealing work, as is elsewhere described as God's so loving the world that He gave His only begotten Son. The giving of the Son by the Father indicates a mystery, a hidden movement in the inner life of the Godhead. But in the self-sacrifice of the man Jesus for His friends, this intra-divine movement is no longer hidden but revealed. For what the man Jesus does . . . is . . . to actualize the human and therefore the visible and knowable . . . aspect of this portion of the divine history. . . . What would the man Jesus be apart . . . from the fact that He is the Revealer of this mystery?

He lives and moves . . . as its Revealer, in the necessary decision and achievement here below of what is decided and achieved by God Himself up above. . . . (III/2, 77; 66)

The earthly history of Jesus is the history in which God has realized His eternal decree in time, and that means, has revealed it. It is the temporal promise of our eternal election, the *revelation* that we *are* already children of God. (II/2, 113; 105f.) It is the event in which God's electing and man's election, both eternal, become visible in time. (II/2, 203; 185) It is Christ's *prophetic* office, the office in which His work becomes a factor in human history. (IV/3, 188–317; 165–274) It is in "the revelation and knowledge of Jesus Christ" that "man and his history are . . . drawn into the history of Jesus Christ." (IV/3, 213f.; 187) "God . . . from all eternity has established the covenant of grace between Himself and man, and has pitied and received him. . . ." To this "the man Jesus" testifies "in time." (III/2, 259; 217)

II

The definitive description of the role of Jesus' temporal history is, therefore, that it is the sign and image of the eternal event of grace.

The earlier volumes of the *Church Dogmatics* call the event in God in which He turns in free decision to a reality outside Himself "revelation." (II/1, 294; 262f.) According to Barth, the human history of Jesus Christ as such is *not* the revelation but is rather the chosen created sign of the revelation. When God speaks to man He chooses a creature to speak for Him. The creature's speech is never God's revelation itself but is rather a sign that revelation is happening. (I/2, 909f.; 814f.) The humanity of Jesus Christ is the primary sign of this sort. (II/1, 223; 199) Even in Jesus' case it holds that a creature can be God's revelation only as the sign of revelation. (I/2, 765; 683)

One entire volume of the *Church Dogmatics* (IV/2) is devoted to the humanity of Christ. Here there is a section (IV/2, 173–293; 154–264) which discusses the nature and significance of Jesus' human life; of this section the second part (IV/2, 185ff.; 166f.) is the material center. Here we have a full and formal definition: "The royal man . . . is created 'after God' (*kata theon*). This means that as a man He exists analogously to the mode of existence of God. In what He thinks and wills and does, in His attitude, there is a correspondence, a parallel in the creaturely world, to the plan and purpose and work and attitude of God." (IV/2, 185f.; 166) In His temporal existence the Son of man *copies* the humiliation of the Son of God; He exists in *conformity* with God's poverty in this world. (IV/2, 186–91; 167–71) His life for man *mirrors* and *reproduces* God's solidarity with man. (IV/2, 200ff.; 179ff.)

When Barth talks here about God's "intent" and "conduct," about the humiliation of the Son, God's poverty in this world and God's love for man, he is not speaking abstractly but about the eternal event of God's decision. This becomes clear when later in the same volume he says that the two qualities of Christ's human life are His humility and His exaltation and analyzes them as follows: God's intent is to condescend to sinful man, to sacrifice Himself for the world. To this end the Father sends the Son and the Son is obedient to the Father. The temporal life of Jesus Christ is the fulfillment of this will of God *in that* it is its perfect representation and reproduction. The human life of the

Son *reproduces* God's life, the decision which *is* His life, the decision in which He humbles Himself to man. (IV/2, 392f.; 351f.)

But Jesus Christ is also exalted on earth. In this He again reproduces the life which God lives in His divine deciding. He reproduces the majesty of the Son's obedience to the Father. In its totality Jesus' life is the witness to that act in God's life in which He turns to His creature. It is the revelation of God's eternal decree. (IV/2, 397–401; 355–9)

"What else is the elect Jesus Christ, the incarnate gratitude of the creature, but the original . . . representation and illustration of the gracious God . . . the true imitator of His work?" (II/2, 457; 413f.)

III

As a result of the pattern we have just described, Barth operates with two viewpoints when he describes the humanity of Christ. On the one hand there is the fact "That the eternal Word as such became flesh. . . ." On the other there is "its attestation through the existence of the man Jesus." (II/1, 58; 53f.) On the one hand there is Jesus Christ's preexistence in God's eternal decree; on the other the "true humanity of Jesus Christ . . . as a history which took place in time," as its "execution and revelation." (IV/2, 33; 31f.) Christ's being as the eternal Son of God is, *also in respect of his humanity,* perfect and complete in God. But it is revealed in time only in a sign—the sign which is His human life. (I/2, 570; 513) Jesus' created life is the sign through which there comes to us dwellers in time—the fact of the accomplished Incarnation. (I/2, 243–53; 223–32)

Perhaps the most remarkable passage in this connection is Barth's discussion of Jesus Christ as the "True Witness." (IV/3, 425–99; 368 434) Barth asks: What is it about this man's life which makes Him the true witness of God's work? He answers: The secret of His power of truth is His unique relation to God. God is unreservedly for Him. He has given His honor as security for the honor of this man. He wills to be God only together with this man. And this man, in all his lowliness, is for God. God's honor is His only honor. Only with God does He wish to be man. (IV/3, 437ff.; 378ff.) Here we have the true God, God as He really is. And here we have the true man. Their meeting, the coincidence of this God's revelation and this man's confession, is the truth. Jesus Christ lives in the power of truth because He lives in this meeting, because in Him the true God and the true man are one. (IV/3, 439–43; 379–83)

But then Barth goes on to say that what he has thus far described is the *pure visage* of the man Jesus Christ, of the True Witness. He has described Him as He is mediator and prophet. But this pure visage is the *hidden* center of His life, His form as it is hidden in God. In this form "He exists for God and before God as his *eternal* Word which became flesh, as his *eternal* Son, who is also the Son of man." (IV/3, 449; 388) He does not wear this pure visage among us. In that He works in our time and among and for us He lives "in a very different form of existence," one adapted to the place of His work and to us men as the receivers of His message. Only God sees Him in His pure visage; among us it is present only as the hidden secret of the face we see. "As He is among us . . . here and now," He bears a visage which hides His presence, the form of the suffering Jesus. (IV/3, 449f.; 389) As the eternal Word, as God sees Him, He would be and remain alien to us. (IV/3, 456; 395)

We may summarize the distinction Barth makes here as that between the eternal Son who is also man and the man who is also the eternal Son. In both cases He is the man Jesus Christ. But in the one case we see Him as the eternal basis of salvation, in the other as the temporal reflection and revelation of the One in whose existence salvation happens.

IV

At this point it is possible that some may be well on their way to supposing that Barth dreams of a sort of self-contained salvation history in eternity, which is then more or less on second thought revealed and reproduced in time. This would be entirely erroneous.[15] To avoid this misinterpretation we must stop and remind ourselves of several points.

We must first remember that Jesus Christ in His temporal life is not the sign and mirror of some other reality but rather a sign of himself. (II/1, 63; 58) He is both a sign and "at the same time the thing signified." (II/2, 62; 58) We must next remind ourselves that the eternal history of which the temporal history of Jesus is the witness and reproduction is first of all a *decision*—the decision that precisely this witnessing and reproducing should take place! The dialectic which Barth evokes here is easy to lose hold of but it is central to this thought. The beginning of all things different from God is a choice made by God. *What* He chooses is that there be a demonstration that He has made such a choice. God wills a creature, precisely to be

[15] It would mean also that we had been looking at the whole matter with that view from the side in which we falsely objectify our relation to revelation—a bad thing in itself and an especially bad place from which to view Barth.

the witness of His glory, the glory which is real in His sovereign choosing. (II/2, 152f.; 184f.; 140ff.; 168ff.) That Gods wills to communicate and reveal Himself and His glory is His primary and basic intention over against His creation. (II/2, 151; 140)

Thus Jesus as the God-man is indeed with God before all time. But He is there only as the chosen man, chosen to no other task than that of witnessing in time. (II/2, 124ff.; 116ff.) On the one hand the man Jesus Christ eternally preexists as the eternal decision in which God is who He is. On the other hand He is "merely" the revealer and reproduction of this decision. But the "merely" is out of place, for Jesus' earthly role as mirror and revealer is an essential expression of the nature of the eternal decision—which is exactly that such a mirroring of itself exist! Jesus is eternally preexistent with God only in the decision in which He is chosen as the revealer of this decision. Christ's temporal history is indeed the mirror of His eternal history, but it is also its purpose! (II/2, 544f.; 490f.)

The witnessing life on earth of Jesus Christ belongs therefore to that to which witness is born. It is "a witness of revelation which itself belongs to revelation. . . ." (I/2, 555; 501) Jesus witnesses to the act of God which happens in His own existence.

We must also remind ourselves that while the eternal history includes God's self-opening to the attack of evil and His victory over it, so that it is indeed an internal occurrence of the whole history of salvation, it is all this only because it is God's choice that there be a revelation of His glory in time. Only because Jesus' earthly life is willed is God involved with evil. (II/2, 185f.; 169f.) God chose his Son to be a creature; as a creature his Son is but the mirror of what God suffered and did—because He chose His Son to be a creature. (II/2, 130ff.; 122ff.)

What happens in time is indeed only a mirror of that to which God eternally opened Himself—in willing that there be such a mirror! Thus the earthly life of Jesus, the sign and mirror of the eternal decree, is not extraneous to His decree, is not an afterthought. This does not mean we repudiate what is already established. The full content of salvation is real in Christ's eternal history and mirrored in His history in time. But the two must not be separated; the eternal history is what it is only in that it is so mirrored. It is exactly the secret of the history in time.[16]

[16] It seems likely that Emil Brunner (*Dogmatics*. vol. I, pp. 346ff.) has overlooked this and sees Barth's doctrine of the preexisting God-man as mythological. There is something in it when Brunner says: "In the New Testament the new element is the fact that the eternal Son of God *became* man, and that henceforth . . . in Him humanity has *received* a share in the heavenly glory; yet in this view of Barth's, all this is now anticipated, as it were, torn out of the sphere of history, and set within the pre-temporal sphere. . . ." (p. 347) But that Brunner is nevertheless criticizing a different view than Barth in fact holds becomes clear when he says: "No special proof is required to show . . . that no theory of this kind has ever been formulated by any theologian." If he had kept the side of the matter we have just discussed in mind he would have realized this is not so. (For a brief glance at the history see Küng, pp. 130–8, 277.) One should not say in so undifferentiated a manner: "If the eternal pre-existence of the God-man were a fact then the Incarnation would no longer be an *Event* at all. . . ." (p. 342)

On the other hand, Bouillard's answer to Brunner, though perhaps correct, seems to me to blunt the point of Barth's thought. "Barth does not suppress the historical event of Jesus; he affirms its eternal presupposition. That which eternally pre-exists before history is the *Verbum incarnandum*, which does not exist except as the object of the divine decree. But . . . Brunner's mistake is excusable, for Barth's text is not entirely clear." (vol. II, p. 154) Barth seems to me to be perfectly clear at this point. Of course, the God-man preexists in the eternal decree in that it is there decreed that He shall exist in time. But it is exactly the nature of the event of the eternal decree which the doctrine of Christ's preexistence intends to determine.

In the other direction, but from the same oversight, Regin Prenter speaks too quickly of Jesus' human life as "merely" the mirror of eternal reality. "In Barth's doctrine of reconciliation Jesus' humanity merely has the role of being a medium through which God's eternal self-love and the election of man concluded therein can be revealed here in time." (*Umbildung*. . . . p. 65) That is quite correct. But the "merely" needs careful qualification. It is not clear without further ado that this is a *criticism* of Barth.

V

A brief closing summary is in order. Jesus Christ's earthly life is the sign and reproduction of the secret of that life. He is the visible image of the act of God hidden in His existence, of His own being as it moves in the eternal counsel of God. We have just seen that this mirroring is essential to His being as eternally preexistent. But we must also remember that it is essential only as sign and reproduction. The eternal election, in which all the content of salvation history already is real, is God's choice before and above all time. *Then,* as sign and reproduction, it occurs also in time. The "eternal communion" of God and man remains the foundation.

"God wills . . . a history, a history in which the share of freedom which [the creature] has already acquired . . . will be attested and proclaimed and apprehended: . . . the share in the sentence which He has pronounced upon it from all eternity. . . ." (III/3, 90f.; 79f.)

Jesus Christ as the Foundation of Creation

The Church has always dutifully taught that all things were created "in" Christ. But in most theology the meaning of that "in" remains utterly obscure. In most theology the doctrine of creation in Christ remains a formal assertion with no content. Through his doctrine of the eternal occurrence of the divine-human life of Christ Barth is able to give meaning to the assertion in a way unprecedented in the history of theology. For Barth, Jesus Christ, the Savior of sinners, precedes creation and is its basis. (II/2, 86, III/1, 82, IV/1, 54; 80, 76, 51f.)

I

The creation, both in its origins and in its historical reality, is the *outer basis* of the covenant with sinners. If we may call this statement the first half of Barth's doctrine of creation, then the second half is: the covenant is the *inner basis* of creation. (III/1, 258–377; 228–329)

This proposition asserts that the covenant which is going to happen is the goal of creation. But it asserts far more than that. For Barth, reconciliation in the mode of predestination precedes creation. Reconciliation is the prior reality; the creation is the beginning of the revelation of that reality.

Creation, says the Bible, is done through Jesus Christ. Barth interprets: Creation is done as part of the carrying out of that relationship between God and man which eternally occurs in the preexistence of the God-man Jesus Christ. And He makes this interpretation plastic: The presence before God of his Son *as a creature* was what motivated him to create. We have seen that creation was an act of God's love. Now we can understand the inner reality of this. God loves His Son; in that His Son is eternally a creature, God loves the creature and in loving it wills its existence. (III/1, 59; 55f.) But we have also seen that the love in which God created was not a love in general, but love for *that* creature who would rebel and sin. Now we can understand the inner reality of this also. In that His Son stands eternally before God as the one who gives himself for fallen man, who *is* fallen man, God loves fallible man. Indeed, He loves the man who must certainly become fallen man. And in loving him He creates him. (III/1, 53f.; 51f.)

If by the Son or the Word of God we understand concretely Jesus, the Christ, and therefore very God and very man, as He existed in the counsel of God from all eternity and before creation, we can see how far it was not only appropriate and worthy but necessary that God should be the Creator. If this was God's eternal counsel in the freedom of His love, the counsel actualised in the manger of Bethlehem, the cross of Calvary and the tomb of Joseph of Arimathea, it was not merely possible but essential for God to be the Creator. God's regard to his Son—the Son of man, the Word made flesh—is the true and genuine basis of creation. (III/1, 54; 51)

The creation, as we saw in the previous chapter, is the presupposition of reconciliation. But it is not only the presupposition of something which is going to happen; it is already the first step in the revelation of that reconciliation which has *already* happened in the preexistence of Jesus Christ. The creature comes to exist in that God's eternal decree begins to be revealed. Creation is, therefore, one great preparation for grace. Its destiny to be in covenant with God is not an addition to its nature; it completely shapes it. Creation is not only the promise but the prefiguration and sign of the Covenant. (III/1, 260–5; 229–34) The primary object of the story of creation is the history of Jesus Christ. Only then is it the history of Israel as a sign of Christ, and only then of the creature as such, as a sign of Israel and Christ. (III/1, 258–377; 228–329)

The creature owes not only its nature but its very existence to God's eternal act of election. The creature could have been nothing. That it is real it owes to God's affirmation of it and to the fact that this is the same affirmation in which God eternally affirms himself. (III/1, 395; 344f.) Creation is not a neutral "making"; it is God's *choosing* of the creature. The God of grace grants reality to the creature. He shows it mercy. "It is *permitted* to be. This is the more precise Christian formulation of the existence of the Creator and the creature. . . ." (III/1, 417; 364)

II

Now we can fully understand what Barth says about the creature's position "on the edge of nihility." God made the creature the threatened creature, the creature who in himself is not equal to the threat of nothingness. But this does not mean that God put the creature in an untenable position. The election of Jesus Christ conquers the problem of created existence, and it precedes that existence. (II/2, 135; 126) God's creation of a world which has all the contradictions of joy and suffering which Barth calls the "shadow side" is justified because He Himself suffered and overcame this contradiction before the creature was subjected to it. (II/2, 180f., III/1, 437; 165f., 381) Indeed, the real inner contradiction of created existence, of the existence of what must be without being God, has been experienced by God alone. He has taken it upon Himself before all time. What the creature experiences is only the representation of the real anguish. (III/1, 436; 380f.)

Now we can fully understand what Barth means by saying that the imperfection of creation is good. The shadow side is good because it mirrors, in creation, the victory which is the basis of the creature's existence. It is the picture within creation of the nothingness to which the creature *might have been* delivered, the picture of nihility as *that which from all eternity has been overcome.* (III/1, 149f.; 133–5) The failures and sufferings of human life are the analogy of *overcome evil.* (IV/1, 398; 360f.)

III

To be a creature means, therefore, to be in Jesus Christ. Our life occurs in that Jesus Christ occurs. Barth has even said: "Anthropological . . . assertions arise only as they are borrowed from Christology." (II/1, 166; 148f.) Of course he does not mean that we can read off a description of man from the doctrine of Christ; Christ is man in a different way than we are men. But what shows us how completely our life is grounded in His—just because we exist—is just the differences between us: Humanity is first Christ's nature and then and therefore ours. What is human is first decided in the eternal decree by which He was chosen for crucifixion and resurrection. That the Son becomes man does not mean that He takes part in a human nature which was there before He assumed it. Rather He determines His own nature and this then *is* human nature. (III/2, 58, 69; 50, 59)

His human nature is not perverted as ours is. In itself His humanity is subject to temptation. But He, man as He is, is also the Creator, the victor over chaos. (III/2, 69f.; 59f.) Moreover, He is not sinless for His own sake, but for ours. His sinlessness is exactly His perfect obedience to the Father, who orders Him to take our sins on Himself. His sinlessness is therefore the foundation of the preservation of our human nature in spite of fall and sin. (III/2, 54–6; 47f.)

The whole structure of human life, and its very existence, is thus based on the fact of Jesus' existence. What makes us be is that in the midst of us there is the man Jesus. (III/2, 158; 132) Every man is defined as the fellow man of Jesus. (III/2, 159;

134) Human being is being which *originates* in the event of its rescue from perversion and its exaltation into fulfillment in the existence of Jesus Christ.[17]

[17] Perhaps it will be useful to introduce Bouillard's correction of the objections Emil Brunner (in *Der Neue Barth*) makes to Barth's anthropology. Bouillard's clear presentation can reinforce our discussion and gather some strands which my train of thought necessarily separates.

Brunner has two objections: (1) ". . . on the one hand the real man is the man who corresponds to God's Creator-will, who affirms God's designation. On the other hand the real man is the one who in fact exists, the sinner who says anything but 'Yes' to God's designation." (pp. 92f.) (2) "Perhaps an ambiguous use of the word 'designation' [*Bestimmung*] plays in. . . . To be sure, the sinner cannot by sinning lose the designation which belongs to his creation. But then 'designation' is something which stands in contradiction to reality. . . . Also in Barth one can read statements like: the man designated *for* life with God, man understood according to that *for which* he is created. But opposing this there are all the other expressions . . . that the real man really does God's will . . ., and that just this man of Creation is that continuum which even by sin is not done away with." (pp. 95f.)

Bouillard lays down the rule: "To comprehend [Barth's anthropological propositions] one must never lose hold of the viewpoint that they have their center in the Barthian doctrine of predestination. . . . man's being reposes in the divine election." Then he responds to Brunner: (1) "The contradiction disappears if one takes the point of view of predestination, as Barth intends. The real man is the one whom God has chosen in Jesus Christ and predetermined to be his partner. This man is in himself necessarily a sinner, but in Jesus Christ he is just." (2) "His destiny to the covenant is through Jesus Christ an accomplished reality and constitutes the ontological definition which makes him the real man. . . . It is from this point of view that Barth identifies the two senses of the word '*Bestimmung*' ('designation') with which he plays: 'destiny' and 'definition.'" That is: "Jesus Christ, according to Barth, pre-exists eternally . . . in God's decree, not only as the Word but as the God-man. As such, even before his appearance on earth, he is the basis of human reality." (vol. II, pp. 236–8) "It is the primacy of Christ which constitutes the primary principle of Barthian anthropology." (vol. II, p. 283)

Wingren must also be mentioned here. He maintains (in *Gott und Mensch in der Theologie Karl Barths* and in *Theology in Conflict,* pp. 23–44) that the great contrast for Barth is the metaphysical contrast between absolute and relative being, between God and man as such, and not the biblical contrast between God and sin. Wingren has seen a touchy point in Barth, but he himself achieves only an obvious falsification of Barth's thought. Some statements in *Gott und Mensch* are hard to excuse. It is quite true that for Barth man-as-such is separated from God and needs to be saved. But this must be understood from the ontological primacy of the covenant in Christ. Because the covenant is the prior reality, one can only be a man-as-such by *rebelling* against the covenant, i.e. by sinning.

IV

With this behind us, two more points from Chapter 2 become clear: The first of these is Barth's doctrine that man's created nature is inalienable, that it is not destroyed or altered by sin. Man cannot lose or alter his nature by sinning, since the basis of his nature is just that event in which the possible damage was repaired in advance. Human nature is first Jesus Christ's. He has not lost or perverted it. We are human only because we participate in His nature, because He is man for our sake. And since He is eternally for sinners our sinning does not destroy our fellowship with him—and so not our human nature. (III/2, 58, 330f.; 50, 274f.)

The second point is the basic proposition that creation is the presupposition of reconciliation. We can now see this in its christological reality and say more precisely: Created being is a presupposition of the event of grace, which does not exist independently of that event but only in it.[18]

Man *is* the being called to be together with Jesus. If we ask, "*What* is called?" we have put forth a false question. The sole

---

In view of the wide distribution of *Theology in Conflict* a few more general remarks seem in order and may as well be begun here. It seems to me that Wingren seizes on Barth's admittedly ontological terminology but ignores the systematic center from which this terminology derives its concrete Barthian meaning—the christological doctrine of predestination. From the thus isolated terminology he constructs a "Barth" who exists only in the pages of Wingren's books. This "Barth" bears a crazy-mirror resemblance to the one from Basel. And Wingren's critique of this "Barth" is often extremely acute—and thus has the same crazy resemblance to a genuine critique of the real Barth. He says things which must be considered, but within a general picture of Barth which is wholly false. See the further discussion under note 11 on Chapter 4.

[18] Von Balthasar has stated the pattern in lapidary fashion: ". . . die eigentliche und ursprungliche Setzung Gottes [setzt] im Akt ihrer Setzung sich selber etwas voraus. . . ." (p. 129) Translation seems impossible.

material presupposition of God's choice is God. To be a man is to be chosen to be with Christ; the human characteristics which answer thereto do not precede but follow God's call. (III/2, 180f.; 150f.)

V

The last question is: *What* is man's nature? Man is, in that Jesus Christ is. But what are the characteristics of the nature which has this foundation? We have already had the answer. Created life is the *likeness* and *mirror* of the covenant of grace in Jesus Christ. Both with respect to man's existence in the image of God and to the shadow side of his life we came to this same description. All that remains to add is Barth's description of how human life mirrors the covenant of grace.

Our human nature mirrors our destiny to live together with God in that humanity is essentially cohumanity. We are so made that we cannot live except together with others. It is in our creation as man and woman that this is inevitable. Here the fact that I am essentially made with reference to another is built into my very physical structure. The man whom God created is neither the male nor the female by himself, nor yet a neutral essence of which these are secondary variations. The man whom God created is man and woman together. To be human is to be cohuman. Our human nature corresponds to its foundation in the union of God and man in Jesus Christ in that it is an *analogy* thereof. (III/2, 290ff., 344ff.; 242ff., 285ff.) [19]

To draw things together: Man exists and is what he is in that he lives together with the man Jesus Christ. He lives by virtue

[19] It is always important to remember that Barth does not believe the order of creation can be *deduced* from the order of reconciliation.

of the unity of God and man which is real in Christ, by participating in this unity. And the mode of his participation in Christ's life is that man is the reflection of that life. In this way man too has a history. And in this way his history is ruled by God's. In this way his history unfolds as the temporal image of the eternal movement of God's will.

Nihility

God's decision to create the world and unite it with himself is not a mere "planning" but the concrete reality of Jesus Christ. Indeed, it is *the* event of which the term "history" may be used without qualification. The case is analogous with God's negative decision, with the unwillingness in which evil has its negated reality.

I

We have seen in the previous chapter that evil "is" in a most problematical fashion. It exists only by virtue of God's will that it shall not exist. God's permitting of evil is, like His creating, a destining. In the case of evil God destines it to cease. That is to say, God's "No" is but the reverse of his "Yes." It has no independence over against God's positive will.

But now we can go farther. The superiority of God's "Yes" is not simply a superiority of affirmation over negation. It is not a merely logical superiority. If it were we would have to reckon with a sort of eternal dialectic of "Yes" and "No" in which the question of my own little historical destiny would remain quite open. A general superiority of God's beneficence would be no comfort against the brute fact of the fall. For logic has nothing to say in the face of fact. (II/2, 184ff.; 168ff.) [20] Rather, the nihility which exists as the object of God's condemnation is from all eternity overcome in fact and deed. This overcoming is accomplished in the act in which God takes it on himself and so destroys it. The decree of God, within the negative side of which evil at once exists and is refuted, is not a conjunction of ideas. That decree is Jesus Christ the crucified and risen. Therefore from all eternity evil has only that reality which it has in Jesus Christ. (II/2, 189; 172f.)

It is the destiny of evil to cease. But this is not just its future destiny, it is also its origin. The last word about evil is also the first. To stretch Barth's point a bit: Not only is evil the negative outer basis of reconciliation in Christ, but reconciliation in Christ is the negative inner basis of evil. One may only speak of evil as he looks back to its destruction in Jesus Christ, for only in this destruction is it there at all. (III/3, 421ff.; 364ff.) [21]

Nihility exists in so odd and negative a fashion because the decree of God which permits it to exist is the same event as the election of Jesus Christ, and because this election in turn is the

[20] The Anglo-Saxon will have to adapt himself to Barth's broad—and more or less vague—continental use of "logic."

[21] This is the point which Berkouwer mostly criticizes. He says that grace can only be understood in relation to what it overcomes. If this is badly understood no amount of insistence on grace's supremacy can help. (pp. 180, 193) In Barth's theology evil is always already bracketed by its own overcoming. Accordingly the historical transition from wrath to grace is lost —and with it the true nature of grace. (p. 214)

Barth replies (IV/3, 198–206; 173–80) that Berkouwer, as a good fundamentalist, tends to think always of deductions from general principles and has mistakenly supposed Barth to deduce his theology from a principle of "grace," where what is really involved is the absoluteness of the *history* in which *Jesus,* not "grace," triumphs. The eternal victory over evil does not cancel out the history of sin and grace—for he who says "Jesus" says "history," he speaks of a way travelled and a conflict won.

Barth's reply is just. Though Berkouwer has seen a danger point, he has in fact misinterpreted Barth.

eternal reality of reconciliation. The basis of evil (which thus really has no basis) *is its own overcoming.*

II

Thus, although it would be an erroneous interpretation of Barth to speak of evil as having a basis, it is nevertheless true that he regards Christ's existence as a necessary precondition of our fallen state. As our created being comes from and leads to Christ the eternal God-man, so also our perversion of that being is not independent of our life in Him. Sin is precisely the self-contradiction involved in trying not to be the one who I in fact am in Jesus Christ. (IV/2, 458f.; 408f.) I am the one who I am in Jesus Christ; I exist in that I am chosen to be His brother. I can only attempt to be something else. In this attempt I fall into self-contradiction; this is the fallenness of man. (IV/2, 461; 410) Apart from Jesus Christ's existence there is no sin.

This means more than that our life is rooted in Christ and that if we did not live we obviously could not sin. Christ's existence as the one who suffers God's condemnation comes first; our lostness follows. He stood, in God's eternal decree, before God's judgment; we stand there only in Him. And because He stood there in the condition of disobedient man we are found guilty. (II/2, 824ff.; 738ff.) We are "sinful flesh" only by virtue of our unity with Christ, *the* man in the flesh. (I/2, 49; 44)

God's will is to have mercy on all. That He shuts up all under disobedience is but the reverse of this will. We arrived at this point in Chapter 2. But now we can make it concrete. God has shut all under disobedience in that He has set the name *Adam* as the title over the whole story of human history. We are all one in Adam the transgressor, not in the sense of historical derivation but in God's decree. (IV/1, 566–70; 507–11) But how does God come to put this title over all history? Only by virtue of human history's other and primary title, which reads "The Story of Jesus Christ." Adam is only a preliminary negative image of Jesus Christ; Christ is Adam's model. And humanity's oneness in Adam is the reflex of its oneness in Christ. (IV/1, 570–3; 512–13) [22]

The "supralapsarian" order of sin and grace which we found in Chapter 2 is not the abstract plan of a God who likes to overcome difficulties, but the expression of the absolute primacy of the Crucified and Risen.

III

Our present christological standpoint also gives the decisive insight into the "ontological impossibility" of sin. In the previous chapter, we saw that since God in creating His creatures destines them to partake in reconciliation they therefore have no propensity to sin. Sin is the absurd, the pointless. But it is clear that this does not give the full basis for the *impossibility* (and so the frightfulness) of sin. For no abstract relation of possibility and impossibility can exclude an event, can do anything in the face of the "So what?" of brute fact. It is because man's being is not only destined for but founded on Jesus Christ's victory over evil, it is because sin originates in its own destruction that it is not only inexplicable (as grace is also!) but perverse—that it is ontologically impossible!

In that man is, he is together with and ruled by the man

[22] See also *Christ and Adam.*

Jesus. Therefore he is guarded from the start against evil, despite his own helplessness. "By the very fact of his creation as man he becomes the covenant-partner and the protégé of his Creator, which denies him not only the right but also the possibility of deciding for chaos and darkness. Because from the very outset God stands at his side, his defencelessness is made good by the One who alone can help. . . ." (III/2, 175; 146f.)

Sin is helpless. It cannot achieve its goal, the establishment of a life separated from grace. For grace gets there ahead of it and grace is exactly God's victory over this attempt.[23]

The real impossibility of sin results from the fact that God's eternal decision to save man is not only idea but event. It is Jesus Christ. Sin is doubly impossible, in its own inner rootlessness and in its downfall in Jesus Christ. (IV/1, 560; 502f.)

IV

But let us rush to reassure: Of course Barth knows that evil and sin are all too visible in our lives as creatures of God. He does not mean that sin and evil "aren't really there." But he does mean that they are there in quite a different way than if they had not been eternally conquered. To anticipate the next paragraphs, nihility, as it appears within created history, is the *shadow of its former self,* the *sign of its own defeat.*

The man of sin is the one who died in Jesus Christ, who was eternally done away with in Christ's work. He is essentially a

[23] "Barth sees sin as that reality which in its existence has 'beforehand', from the beginning, been overtaken and therefore can impossibly effect what it wishes and intends to achieve, namely, the nullifying of grace. . . . It is impotent because it is unable to create a really new situation but rather finds expression in that area which is the area of God's grace." (Berkouwer, p. 234)

reality of the past, he is our yesterday. He is the one who we were, not the one who we are or can be. Nor is this true only of the Christian or of those who live after the temporal coming of Christ; this is Barth's definition of the sinner of all times. And if we nevertheless attempt to be men of sin, it is as the revival of our own past, as our own ghosts. (IV/1, 558–61; 501–3)

Nihility is in its essence the antiquated, the fleeting, "the eternal yesterday." (III/3, 410; 355) When God finishes saying "No," what He denies ceases. But this is just what He has done in Jesus Christ, from all eternity. Because of Jesus Christ we must say that nihility does not exist any longer, and that this was always so. This is its essence, not to exist any more. *Post Christum* evil is only an apparent reality; it is the shadow and after-image of what it was. And the time when nihility "was" is the eternal pastness of what God shut out in his eternal decision. The evils and sins which seem sometimes to make up human history are exactly this appearance, this after-glow of a vanished glare. Nihility itself has no constitutive meaning for human history. (III/3, 416–25; 360–8)

The sole recourse of nihility, *post Christum*, is the attempt to hinder our knowledge of our reconciliation with God, to create an illusion. (IV/3, 299f.; 259ff.) It is in its form as untruthfulness, as the *lie*, that sin is a factor in human history. (IV/3, 430; 372f.)

V

What is the temporal reality of evil? The answer is before us. It is its own shadow, its own after-image. All man's efforts fail to conjure up more than this ghost of original evil. (III/1, 120;

108f.) "In and with the lie there comes into view and action again the man who in Jesus Christ, and therefore in the eternal election and historical act of God, has been . . . put to death, i.e., the man of sin. . . . As man lies he conjures up the shade of this dead man. . . ." (IV/3, 534; 464)

Once and once only nihility becomes real in history, in the crucifixion of Jesus Christ. Only Christ's death is really an experience of God's judgment.

> Knowing neither sin nor guilt, He caused this judgment to fall on Himself in place of the many guilty sinners, so that it availed for them all, and the judgment suffered by Him was fulfilled on them in Him, and their dying no longer has to be this dying, this suffering of punishment which they have deserved, but only its sign. (III/2, 730; 600)

Our corruption, the decomposition of our lives in their contradiction to their own reality, is something which only Jesus Christ has really experienced. What we experience is the shadow of His cross. To be sure, it is *our* collapse which He experiences; we are the ones engaged in self-destruction. What we experience is but the reminder of "the misery of which He has made an end in His death . . .," a sign that we will *not* have to experience dissolution. (IV/2, 551; 487f.)

In sum, the wrath of God has happened but once, at the Crucifixion. All other historical manifestations of God's anger are but copies and signs of the real thing. (II/1, 445f.; 395f.) They are the signs that God's wrath does *not* strike us; since they occur in time they cannot be more. (II/1, 472f.; 419f.) Even the Crucifixion is a primary occurrence of wrath only because it is not only a temporal event.

Eternal History and the Life of Faith

Finally, what of Christian life? What of our lives as those who know that Christ is eternally and temporally the bond between God and ourselves? [24]

I

The life of the Christian is based upon the eternal primacy of Jesus Christ. Barth sums up the content of God's work in our lives in the two concepts "justification" and "sanctification." (IV/1, 140ff.; 128ff.) He defines these in turn as functions of one basic occurrence, "participation in Christ." (IV/2, 578; 510f.) Christ is both our righteousness and our holiness; we are righteous and holy in that we are His. But how can Jesus' righteousness and holiness count for us? How can it really be ours? That which is Christ's can be and is ours because He is the foundation of our lives, because from the very beginning we *are* what we are in Him. (IV/2, 303; 273f.) It is the ontological foundation of all men's lives in Jesus which makes literal truth of the proclamation: "You are holy and good for Jesus' sake." (IV/2, 305; 275) Within God's will, Jesus' humanity is that of all men, so that what is true of Him is true of all. (IV/2, 586–9; 518–21)

II

This eternal foundation in Jesus Christ of our life with God transcends all that happens in time. It transcends the historical

[24] Plainly we cannot discuss Barth's whole pneumatology. I will only isolate those points which are important for our line of thought.

preaching and hearing of the Gospel. It transcends the historical act of coming to faith. (II/2, 352f.; 321ff.) According to Barth, none of these is the basis of Christian life.

Then what does the Church do when it tells of Christ? According to Barth it witnesses to a state of grace which is in no way dependent on this witness. It witnesses to an eternally accomplished election. It tells men what they already are. (II/2, 350f.; 318ff.)

And what is the earthly life of the Christians, of those whom God gathers through this witness? It is a human life and history in which there occurs a visible representation of God's life and history. (II/2, 457; 413f.) To what does God call us through the Gospel? To be the image of Christ, to "manifest and reproduce and reflect" the life of the *one* called of God. (II/2, 382; 347) [25] Therefore faith has no fundamentally creative character. It is a *cognitive* event.[26] Faith is the *confirmation* in my daily life of the change in the human situation which has already occurred. (IV/1, 839f.; 751f.) [27] When I come to faith I do not thereby become a new creature, I do not thereby enter into the covenant with God. I *realize* that I am a new creature, that God has made covenant with me. The event of faith is not an eschatological decision; I do not decide my eternal destiny when I decide for faith. *I* do not decide my eternal destiny at all. The eschatological decision is God's act in Jesus Christ; faith is the human decision

[25] The same, in negative form, is said of those who are *rejected* in this world.

[26] As an act of man. As an event in which *God* is at work it has, in *effect*, a creative character. See Küng, pp. 88–94, 253ff. But it must be noted that what is created is precisely the new subject who is capable of this *knowledge*.

[27] Notice that the same dialectic we found in the discussion of Christ's human life repeats itself here. For the alteration which occurs prior to faith is such that this confirmation *must* take place.

and act which God thereby makes possible. (IV/1, 857ff.; 767ff.)

What then is faith? It is the analogy of God's act in Jesus Christ. The Christian is the one who can no longer live except in imitation of Jesus' death and resurrection, whose human life has become in its own small way a dying and rising again. (IV/1, 859f.; 768f.) Faith is trust in God, and so an analogy of God's trustworthiness. (IV/1, 709; 634f.) It is the obedience of humility, and so the analogy of Jesus' whole life. (IV/1, 709f.; 635f.)

And what are the works of love which follow faith? They are that which "in respect of our existence which now is and passes, by its very nature 'can only' be the erecting of a sign. . . ." (I/2, 453; 410)

In summary: The whole history of the preaching of Christ's Gospel on earth and of the faith which it awakens is a decision "corresponding to what is decreed in heaven and not on earth, by the counsel of God and not by the apostles or the Church, that is, by the everlasting decree for the world, in Jesus Christ." (II/2, 490; 442)

Summary

The eternal origin of the events of human history is not a static "Being," nor is it the forming of a "plan" of salvation by a puzzled or ingenious God. The eternal origin of the temporal history of salvation is nothing other than that history itself in its own deepest character as an event in the life of the eternally active God. It is thus a weak expression to say that God "guides the history of salvation"; He *is* that history in its primary and most truly historical reality.

Now inasmuch as this history in God is, by His grace, a history of His turning to men, this history appears also in time. The word, "appears," in the last sentence is precise. The temporal history of salvation is the appearance to us of our own inner history before God. Indeed, all our history is this. Despite its inner differentiation into human history as such and the special history of revelation, human historical reality is as a whole the appearance outside of God and the reflection back to Him of the glorious love which eternally happens in the life of the One who unites Himself with man in Jesus Christ.

This is a disturbingly radical answer to our second question: "In what sense is God himself involved in 'history'? And how does His history control ours?" But for the moment let us simply try to live with it and continue on to our third question.

CHAPTER FOUR

CHRIST THE ALPHA AND THE OMEGA

The Problem

I

Any doctrine which claims to open up to men the meaning and purpose of their lives is necessarily also a description of reality. The Christian Gospel is no exception. If it says to me that Jesus Christ is the center of everything it thereby says that everything has Jesus Christ at its center and so makes a decisive statement about the nature of what is real. It is not idle speculation but simply an unfolding of the concrete attachments of the Gospel to life, when we go on to ask what "everything" must be *like* to have Jesus Christ at its center. Therefore, theology as the science of this proclamation necessarily becomes a struggle with the old question of what things are really like. Any particular theological system or approach will at least presuppose and imply certain convictions on this matter. Our pet cliché, "Christianity is an historical religion," seems to make some blessedly vague assertion about this, to say that what Christian faith perceives as real is not the timeless but what *happens*. But this only raises the desperate question: "*What* happens?" It raises the third question we must direct to Barth.

Again, Christian talk is plainly *about* something.[1] Any theology, insofar as it is a unified and intelligible body of proposi-

[1] At least for Barth. And, I think, for all who actually use this talk.

tions, will embody some view of the nature of the putative reality to which its propositions refer. What is Barth's view of the reality to which theology testifies?

II

The need for this chapter can also be discovered within Barth's thought. What we have presented in Chapters 2 and 3 never appears so neatly divided in Barth's own writing. The two questions we have directed to him: "What is the plan of history as God rules it?" and "What is the mode of God's rule of history?" are questions which Barth never asks separately. And the answers we found: "The coming of Christ to sinners is absolutely determined from all eternity and is the purpose of all that happens," and "Christ's life, as a movement of God's eternal will, is itself the basis of its appearance in time," are for Barth one and the same proposition.[2] Clearly we must spend some time making explicit to ourselves the unity which these two topics have for Barth, for if we allow them to fall apart the results are disastrous.

In his discussion of the controversy between the old supralapsarians and infralapsarians Barth speaks of the demonic appearance which the supralapsarian God so easily acquired. (II/2, 151; 140) If Barth's description of the divinely ordained course of salvation history stood alone in his thought his God would also have a demonic appearance. For the God who created men in a hopeless situation in order at some later date to show off what a great rescuer He was would be scarcely less merciless than the old Calvinist God whose sole concern was the salvation of Jones and the damnation of Smith.

[2] See *Christ and Adam*.

If Barth's "supralapsarianism" were an independent complex of thought it would be a great abstraction of the idea of grace from its reality in Jesus Christ. The old supralapsarians show how the abstracted idea of grace constantly threatens to turn into its own opposite. Barth is not guilty of this abstraction. When he speaks of "grace" he means Jesus Christ. His supralapsarianism is always embedded in the doctrine of the primacy of the concrete person of Christ.

On the other side, a doctrine of Christ as the foundation of all things could also be a vicious abstraction. If we were to develop it apart from the dialectic of sin and forgiveness we would end with a "Jesus Christ" as the basis of our lives who was not the Jesus Christ of Bethlehem and Golgotha.

Even when we isolated Barth's doctrine of Christ's primacy we saw that it was not such an abstraction. It was the crucified and risen Christ whom Barth called the origin of all things. The eternal history in God's bosom is *salvation* history.

Thus the motifs of the last two chapters are only the inner determinants of one unified view of reality. Only so does each have its true function and avoid the perversion which it would suffer by itself. We must now turn explicit attention to this unity.

Created Reality and Reconciled Reality

What then is the common meaning of our two questions and two answers? It is this: Under God's sovereignty in Jesus Christ there is only one order of reality. Reality is not divided into what "is" and what "happens" to it. Nor is reality divided into two orders of events: into "secular" and "religious" orders or into orders of creation and reconciliation. To be sure, creation and reconciliation can be distinguished, but they are never present separately. They are *inner* determinants of one great order of reality—which is at once an order of creation and an order of reconciliation, a secular order and a religious order, "being" and "history."

I

To begin at the simplest level, Barth does not teach a temporal succession of the orders of creation and reconciliation. A "pure" creature, a creature who was not also a fallen creature, has never existed; the order of creation has never been the sole order. "There never was a golden age. . . . The first man was immediately the first sinner." (IV/1, 567; 508) "Adam's fall" is not an event which was preceded by other events; it is a basic *structure* of all human history. (IV/1, 567; 508f.) The story of paradise does not describe an original goodness of the creature but points to the original will of God, in the conflict between God and man which is the sole history of the creature. (III/1, 239; 212) Nor was there ever a created and fallen man who was not involved in the history of reconciliation. "As created by God, human reality has been embraced by God and his covenant from all eternity." (III/2, 661; 546) Nor is this a general truth which must *become* valid for particular men; it is valid for all. (II/1, 176; 157f.) The temporal event of reconciliation is the confirmation of a threatened but existing fellowship. (IV/1, 71; 67) When faith sees reconciled man, when it confesses the reality of the history in which man is justified, it sees and confesses this for all men and as the secret of all history. (IV/1, 685; 614)

II

Nor are the orders of creation and reconciliation merely contemporary. God's work as Creator and his work as Reconciler are bound to each other in the closest possible way. Indeed, His grace as the Reconciler is nothing other than faithfulness to His work as Creator—and vice versa.

As man's Creator, in His faithfulness as such, and as He thus gives persistence and constancy to man and his sphere, God is also his Reconciler. . . . If what He does as the Founder and Lord of this covenant is not the same as what He does as Creator, He does not do either without the other, but does both simultaneously and in co-ordination: The work of His creative grace has in view [*gezielt auf*] His reconciling grace. But the converse is also true. . . . (IV/3, 156f.; 138)

So there is a realm of nature which as such is distinguished from the realm of grace. But everything in nature has its origin and goal in grace. And in turn the realm of grace contains nothing unnatural. (III/1, 67; 62) Let us try to make this mutuality of God's two works more precise.

Barth summarizes his anthropology by saying that man's being is a history. What history? Barth answers: It has happened that God has accepted man by becoming a man himself. This event is the inner core of all else that happens; it is primary history.[3] In the deepest sense only Jesus, who is this man, is history. But there are other men, as those who are together with Jesus. This is their very being—*their involvement in Jesus' history*. Apart from this they would have no history but would be static and so would not exist. (III/2, 188–93, 203; 157–62, 170)

[3] *Urgeschichte*.

Therefore the content of the history in which man has his being is the call of God's saving grace. Man *is* the creature who is broken out of himself and set into movement by meeting God's grace. Man *is* in that the God of grace calls him; he exercises his being in that he follows the call and lives in dependence on that grace. (III/2, 196–8; 164–6)

What is the history which is man's being? It is his involvement in the history of salvation in Jesus Christ. The act of God by which He gives man being is no other act than the act by which He saves him. Man exists by virtue of the power of God's pledge and promise to be his helper and savior. Man exists in that God comes to him through His word, in that he is opened up to God. He is founded on God's word of grace. He is "the being which responds and is complementary to that grace." (III/2, 200; 168)[4]

So much for man's creation. With his continuing history the case is even clearer. We have seen that here too we must distinguish two realms which correspond exactly to creation and reconciliation. We must distinguish the history of the creature as such from the history of God's saving work. But when Barth discusses the acts of God which sustain and rule these histories he says that God "sustains" human life in general in that He

[4] "One sees that two motifs mark Barth's definition of man as a creature of God. First, man's being does not consist of a 'nature,' corporeal or spiritual; it is really an act, a history. Second, this act depends completely from God's saving act in Jesus Christ. We do not possess our true being in ourselves but only in this that God has loved us, loves us and will love us." (Bouillard, vol. 2, p. 235) For a full examination of this point in Barth's thought see Bouillard, vol. 2, pp. 219–86.

It is at this point that Roman commentators in general become nervous. All are concerned that to the acts of God's creation and grace there ensue a creaturely being and state of grace which can be separately described as the reality of the creature—and see this threatened by the "narrowness" with which Barth ties nature to grace. Besides Bouillard, see: Volk, *Die Christologie bei Karl Barth und Emil Brunner*. pp. 614–43; and Balthasar, pp. 139–48, 335–98. Küng is more satisfied with Barth's position. (p. 44)

sustains life in faith. (III/3, 95; 83f.) His will in which He "accompanies" His creature is "his fatherly good-will, his decree of grace in Jesus Christ, the mercy in which from all eternity He undertook to save the creature . . ., which as such is also his kingly will, disposing of . . . the existence and activity of the creature." (III/3, 132; 117) God's watch over His creature is His work in the history of the covenant, as this is founded on His decree of grace and fulfilled in the giving of His Son, which then *as such* is also His exercise of power in the whole sphere of His creation. (III/3, 132f.; 117)

The third element of providence is God's "rule" of the creature. According to Barth the one act of God's rule is His word and deed of forgiving grace. There is no other power of God than that at work in the covenant of grace. God rules creation in that this one act of rule reaches beyond its immediate implementation in the history of the covenant to include all other events as well. Therefore the plan and content of the two histories is one and the same. The only difference is that the history of the covenant is the revelation of the content of all history. What is revealed in covenant history is hidden in history as such. (III/3, 222; 196)

III

All of reality derives from and is ruled by the one great work of God. If this is the case, how can Barth speak of two orders at all? Does any difference remain between creation and reconciliation, history in general, and the history of the covenant? God's one work is effective in two areas; His covenant rule reaches out to include all things. But what is the distinction between these two areas of God's work?

To begin, we must be clear that (to continue an inexact figure) the two areas are not separate; one lies within the other. Natural man is present only as reconciled man; if he were not reconciled, if he were left to the consequences of his revolt, neither would he be his natural self. On the other hand, reconciled man is more than natural man. (III/2, 670; 552f.) The man who stands in the covenant of grace is the only actual man; he includes his purely created reality as part of his actual self. Perhaps we could say: "Natural man" is an abstraction from the one factual reality of fallen and reconciled man. Only this is not an arbitrary abstraction but an inner distinction essential to the being of reconciled man.

What is this inner distinction? We have already seen that the order of creation is the "technical" presupposition of reconciliation. But wherein is it a presupposition? What role does natural man play? Wherein is it an essential inner distinction of reconciled man to have within himself this presupposition of his reconciled existence?

We approach this question through an examination of one of the most interesting places in Barth's theology. Barth maintains that death is natural for man, a part of his existence which God created good. His discussion is interesting for its own sake and is the classical place for our present problem.[5]

In present fact, death is unnatural, the sign of God's condemnation of the perverted creature. Nevertheless, death, even as judgment, confronts us with God—who is always the God of grace. The judgment of which death is a sign is therefore a judgment based on grace. The curse falls on those who remain

[5] Heinrich Vogel asserts that it is in this discussion that the systematic consequences of Barth's anthropology appear most clearly. (*Ecce Homo*, pp. 114–7)

in the covenant. Death as we now experience it is the judgment which takes everything from us—in order that God may be our sole hope. (III/2, 722ff.; 593ff.)

This is true only in Jesus Christ. Only in Him is God our hope even in death. Only in Him is death only the *sign* of final condemnation. But we *are* in Him and therefore have hope. (III/2, 746–9; 613–6)

So we have hope even in the death we now know. But this is still not what Barth set out to show. We still have not seen how death is natural; it still remains the sign of judgment over fallen man. We must go on.

So far we have equated the end of life with "death." And factually they are indeed identical. A different end of life has never happened and is not even conceivable. In Jesus' death we see this conclusively. But—and this is the decisive point in Barth's argument—in Him we also see that the identity of "death" and life's end is not built into human nature. He would have been no less human if He had not "died," if He had not suffered that end which is the sign of God's wrath. That He ended His life by dying is something—so the Gospel has always proclaimed—He died for our sakes, not for His own. It follows that He would not have needed to "die," but could have ended His life otherwise without ceasing to be true man. (III/2, 764–6; 627–9) Moreover, because of His death our death has become only the sign of judgment, only the sign of what it might have been. And so we learn that our end too could have been different, could have been something other than "death." Neither for Christ nor, in Him, for us, is the need to end life by dying one of the constants which make us men. (III/2, 767; 630)

Jesus' death was grace; He would not have had to "die." On the other hand, He had to be *able* to die in order to show this grace, in order to die for us. The finitude of His life *was* a part of His nature as a man, was a requirement of His humanity, because His humanity was precisely His self-giving for us. And since what happened on Calvary is what is meant by "good," Jesus' finitude, His ability to die, was a good part of His human nature. (III/2, 767; 630)

Our life too must come to an end. For only in this way are we in a position to be finally and utterly dependent upon Jesus Christ someday as the Savior from death. If we were immortal then reconciliation and salvation from death would be meaningless. Therefore finitude is a part of our created nature and a good part of it.

This is Barth's argument. Now we ask: What is meant by "nature" in this context? First, "nature" is factually identical with the order of reconciliation. The "natural" finitude of life is never real except as death, except as judgment and grace. Nor is it even separately conceivable. "Nature" never exists as such. And this is first of all true with Jesus Christ who is the foundation of all humanity.

Second, "nature" appears in the argument as something necessary to the order of reconciliation. It is necessary in order that reconciliation be reconciliation. Barth proves that finitude is "natural" by proving that it is necessary in order that death, in which Jesus wins forgiveness and we receive it, take place.

Third, the concept of "nature" is introduced by Barth just at those points where he wants to show that things could have been different than they in fact are. Natural finitude is postulated in order that death could have been something other than "death."

Fourth, it is as this factor of possibility, as this point where it could have been different, that nature is necessary to the order of reconciliation. Jesus' death has to be possible in order that there be grace. But Jesus' death *is* grace and not a mere catastrophe or natural necessity in that it would not have had to be "death."

I would like to propose that in Barth's theology the order of nature or creation is not a fact but the possibility within the one factual order of reconciliation by which it would not have *had* to be that order. "Nature" is the possibility of an order which would not have been an order of sin and forgiveness. It is the inner determination by which the creature could without self-contradiction have been other than the fallen and reconciled creature. It is the inner freedom without which the order of reconciliation would not be an order of grace but of fate—and so neither reconciliation nor reconciliation of sinners.

To push this interpretation one last step, we now can refer back to the doctrine of God and say: The inner distinction in which the one order of reality is at once an order of creation and an order of reconciliation is the expression in that order of the fact that its Lord is the God who is free in all His works. He is the God of whom it must always be said that He could have done otherwise than He does.

IV

This discussion is best concluded by citing the formulas in which Barth has summarized his own thinking and brought it to final clarity. These formulas have been our silent guides all through this section, indeed all through this study.

> Even the formal and general truth must be considered that God and man are in any case bound and live *together*. As Jesus Christ lives, God and man live in this conjunction. . . . This is the epitome of the whole order of creation. This order too, has its dignity, validity,

power and persistence in the fact that Jesus Christ lives. But it has its content and fulness in the fact that the life lived by Jesus Christ is the life of grace, that it is the life of the Saviour. From the standpoint of this content . . ., the one order of God is the order of reconciliation. . . . The eternal meaning and content of the order of creation are worked out in the one order of God in the fact that this order is also that of reconciliation. The unity of the two . . ., or, as we might say, the unity of the form and content of the one order of God, is event and reality in the fact that Jesus lives. (IV/3, 45f.; 43)

In these statements we see the final meaning of the doctrine that the creation is the outer basis of the covenant and the covenant the inner basis of creation. The difference between the order of creation and the order of reconciliation, between nature and grace, is the difference between form and content of one order of reality.

Inclusive Christology

These same citations bring us to our next topic. Nature, grace, and the unity of the two are real in that Jesus Christ lives. To complete our study we must investigate Barth's Christology.

We anticipate the result: Barth's Christology is not so much a description of the individual person of Jesus Christ as it is a description of the history of God with man, of the one great event which is all of reality, at its personal center.

I

This is clear from the very beginning of Barth's Christology. He introduces the doctrine of reconciliation by discussing the grace of God and the response of man. Then he arrives at Christology by discussing the mid-point at which these two movements, of God to man and man to God, meet. Jesus Christ, Barth says, *is* this event. He exists in that reconciliation occurs, in that God turns to man and man is converted to God. (IV/1, 133ff.; 122ff.)

Therewith Barth achieves a connection to the classic formulas of Christology: True God, true man, true God-man. In Jesus Christ we have to do with God in His movement to man, with man in his movement to God and with the unity of the two. (IV/1, 138; 126) But at this point Barth breaks out characteristically: "We hasten to explain. . . ." The "being" involved is a history. Jesus Christ "is" God and man only in the event in which God reconciles and man is reconciled. His being as God-man consists in His deed, in His history. And this is the history of the reconciliation of God with man. (IV/1, 138–40; 126–8) Therefore the doctrine of the person of Christ may not be separated from the doctrine of His work. Rather, since He is what He does, the doctrine of His person must be at the same time the doctrine of His work. (IV/1, 139f.; 127f.)

Now the content of the movements which make up Christ's history, and so His person, is humiliation and exaltation. God humbles Himself to man and exalts man to Himself. Since these two movements *are* the two natures in Christ it follows that the doctrine of the "states" of Christ, of His humiliation and exaltation, must also be identical with the doctrine of His person. (IV/1, 145ff.; 132ff.)

With this we have before us the unique structure of the Barthian Christology. In the old Christology there were three divisions: (1) the doctrine of Christ's person, which described, so to speak, His constitution, by virtue of which He is capable of His work of reconciling; (2) the doctrine of the states of Christ, of

His humiliation and exaltation, which described briefly the history in which He performed His work; (3) the doctrine of the work of Christ, which described what He did. In Barth's Christology these divisions are abolished. The doctrines of Christ's person, work, and history collapse into each other. In their place Barth substitutes a division based on the two-natures doctrine. He treats Christ as God, Christ as man, and Christ as God-man.

In this Christology Christ's Godhead is identical with God's work of reconciliation, which in turn is identical with the history in which He works. His humanity is identical with man's response as one who is reconciled, which, in turn, is identical with the history in which man is reconciled. His existence as the God-man is exactly the oneness in which these two histories occur. *That is to say,* for Barth the structure of Christ's being is identical with structure of the history between God and man. It is identical with the structure of the covenant of reconciliation. (IV/3, 2; 4)

"The will of God triumphs in Jesus Christ because He is the way from the heights to the depths, and back again to the heights. . . . God presents this man in omnipotent loving-kindness as His Elect and Himself as the God who elects this man. Jesus Christ is this irreversible way. . . ." (II/2, 466; 421)

Therefore we can say that Jesus Christ "is" the God-man only if we immediately interpret this "is" with a "becomes." The Incarnation is never a result, never something that God *has* done, never something from which He can move on to other works. Jesus Christ *is* God's work and God's work is Jesus Christ. Therefore the Incarnation is always an event, always to be described with present-tense action verbs. (IV/2, 48f.; 45f.) There is no other being of Christ than the movement of God to man and of man to God. (IV/2, 116–9; 105–8)

II

Within this framework Barth conducts a truly massive development of the christological doctrines. It is impossible to give anything like a fair picture of its fullness or subtlety in these pages.[6] Barth operates with the apparatus of classical Christology: Christ is one person in two natures. He is the God-man, He is God, He is man. For all such Christology the two decisive problems are clearly: What is the nature of the unity of God with humanity which is brought about by the fact that the one Christ possesses both natures? And what is the meaning of the assertion that God and man are, in Christ, one and the same *person?* We will sketch Barth's answer to each of these questions in turn.

In a formal sense, Barth defines the relation of Christ's divine and human natures as "participation." (IV/2, 67; 62f.) The elements of Christ's human nature are all involved in the life of the Son of God and so participate in the divine essence, and vice versa. (IV/2, 69; 64)

Then Barth describes the content of this "participation": In the Son's assumption of human life He has exalted human nature into Himself. This is what is meant by reconciliation, that God lifts humanity into fellowship with Himself. (IV/2, 74f.; 69f.) Here is our first hint as to what is meant by the mutual "participation" of divinity and humanity in Christ; it is the *fellowship* of God and man. Barth then defines this more precisely. Within the one person of Christ both natures are *determined* each by the other. They are mutually preoccupied. No alteration of the human nature occurs. What does occur is its elevation to fellowship

[6] For a fuller discussion see my Heidelberg dissertation, pp. 156ff.

with God, to perfect unanimity with the divine nature. (IV/2, 75–9; 69–72)

Barth then states the content of this mutual preoccupation: "The actuality of the incarnate Son of God, the union of the two natures in Him, is the direct confrontation of the totality of the divine with the human in the one Jesus Christ." (IV/2, 94; 86) God and man are one in Jesus Christ *in that* in Him they are *confronted* with one another and exist under the conditions given in this confrontation. (IV/2, 92–8; 84–9)

What does this confrontation communicate to the divine nature? Barth says: "attention" and "concern" for man, the characteristic of being God with and for man. (IV/2, 92–5; 84–7) And how does this confrontation affect the human nature? It becomes a "human essence" "adopted and controlled and sanctified and ruled" by God (IV/2, 97; 88) It is elevated into "that harmony with the divine will, that service of the divine act, that correspondence to the divine grace, that state of thankfulness, which is the only possibility in view of the fact that this man is . . . brought . . . into . . . direct . . . confrontation with the divine essence." (IV/2, 101; 92) It is given perfect participation in the work of the Holy Spirit. (IV/2, 103–6; 93–6) It is made an organ of God's work, i.e., in its purely human fashion it testifies to and serves that work. The Son alone remains the doer. (IV/2, 106–10; 96–100)

It is plain that the relation between the two natures of Christ, as Barth describes it, is exactly the covenant of grace, as Barth describes it, no more and no less. As he himself says: "It is a matter of covenanting and therefore . . . of God's deed which remains exclusively his. . . ." (IV/2, 112; 101)[7]

[7] See note 14 to Chapter 2.

If we turn to the problem of the existence of God and man as one person we arrive at the same results. Barth says: The life of the Son of God became the life of a man. The Son lives invisibly as God and visibly in this world as a human "thou." When we have to do with Jesus we have to do with God. (IV/2, 53f.; 50f.) This is further explained: The existence of Jesus Christ is "act," i.e. being in spontaneous self-realization. He lives and, as He lives, He freely and spontaneously fulfills the destiny which is His. He lives as God and man. He fulfills His being as God and He fulfills his being as man in one and the same set of deeds and sufferings, in one and the same life-history. As He lives, divine and human self-realization occur together as one event. (IV/3, 42f.; 40f.)

What does Barth mean by "joint self-realization"? By this he means that what Jesus Christ does as the Son of God and what He does as the Son of man He does not only simultaneously but in the strictest correlation of the one to the other. (IV/2, 128; 115) But "joint realization" also means: What Jesus Christ does as the Son of God and what He does as Son of man He does so, that each nature realizes *itself*, the divine as the divine and the human as the human, *Per efficiam distinctam utriusque naturae.* (IV/2, 128; 115)[8] Concretely:

The one Word of Jesus Christ is his self-expression as God's eternal Word, and it is also the corresponding, but not identical, word of the proclamation of this man. . . . The one power of Jesus Christ is the omnipotent power of God and it is also the distinct but fully attesting power, the great and yet limited power, in which this man does signs and wonders. The one death and passion of Jesus Christ is the final depth of the self-humiliation of God and it is also, fol-

[8] It will be plain from what follows that this classic formula, applied to the "Son of God" and the "Son of man," means something quite different than in its older use.

lowing and completing it as a human death and passion, the way which the man Jesus . . . traversed. . . . (IV/2, 129; 116)

In that we have to do with Jesus we have to do with God. What this means concretely Barth defines: "It is in fact the singularity and transcendence of God which finds its creaturely correspondence, reflection and representation in this man. . . ." (III/2, 161; 135)

In short, Barth describes the union of God and man in the one person of Christ in terms which are unmistakably the characteristics of the covenant of grace as he has elsewhere described it. The man Jesus exists in perfect *correspondence* with God. He exists for God and God alone. But God and man remain in absolute contrast; God does His work and the life of the man Jesus testifies to it.[9]

The result, therefore, of examining Barth's answers to the two great problems of Christology is uniform. God and man are one in Jesus Christ; the Son of God is Jesus, and Jesus is the Son of God, *in that* the Son and Jesus are in perfect and unbroken covenant with each other. A "meeting between God and man takes place in the figure of Christ in the New Testament and in this meeting is the event which is the object of New Testament witness, *vere Deus vere homo*." (I/2, 183; 168)

III

How can we make clear the difference between this Christology and classical Christology? Perhaps in this way: Classical Christology saw God's reconciling activity as the divine-human

[9] I do not assert that this is the *whole* reality of the *unio personalis* in Barth's theology. It may be so. Prenter (*Karl Barths Umbildung der traditionellen Zweinaturlehre. . . .*) rather jumps to this assertion. But I would not wish to assert it without more investigation than is in order here.

work of the God-man done on the rest of humanity. Barth sees God's reconciling work as itself the structure and reality of the mediator's existence as God and man. Or again: In the classical Christology God became man in order, *as man,* to perform His divine work on *us*. According to Barth, God works "inside" the person of the mediator, on the man who is present in this person. Once again: In classical Christology God works in and through the human nature of Christ as through His own nature. Here God works *on* the human nature of Christ. Christ is within Himself both subject and object of the work of God.[10]

For classical Christology the history of salvation, the history of Christ and His people, is the history between God-in-Christ and mankind. For Barth's Christology it is the history between God and man as these are present in the two natures of Christ. One almost wants to say without qualification: It is the history *between* the two natures of Christ. The classical Christology was concerned with the history made by the one person of the God-man, with the deeds worked by God-in-Christ. Barth's Christology is concerned with the history worked by God on Jesus, "in" Christ.

IV

The last stop in our analysis comes when we see that for Barth this covenant between God and man, which is the reality of the person of Jesus Christ, is, *as such,* also the covenant between

[10] Here is the key to Barth's ability to join the strongest possible statements of the identity of the Son of God with Jesus of Nazareth with explanations in terms of "fellowship," "correspondence," and the like—a characteristic confusing to one who comes from the traditional discussions. The transposition of the history between God and man "inside" the person of Jesus Christ gives the classical terminology Barth uses a whole new location. The classical propositions acquire entirely new meanings.

God and all men. The history which, as His interior history constitutes the person of Christ, is at the same time the history of God's covenant with all men—and so finally the entire history of God with His creation.

Barth teaches, as do all Christian theologians, that God's covenant with man is fulfilled in Jesus Christ. But this has a very particular meaning for Barth. For him, the fulfillment of the covenant in Christ means that in His person the covenant is a complete and accomplished history, that in His single person God, man, and the history between them are completely present. (IV/3, 184f.; 161ff.) This covenant in Jesus Christ (the word "in" very nearly means "inside") is then, *as such,* God's covenant with the rest of us. This history between God and man in the person of Christ is, *as such,* God's history with mankind.

As Barth develops the doctrine of reconciliation in three great divisions he begins each division with Christology. In each case this is concluded by a section which makes the transition to an anthropological section. (IV/1, 311–94, IV/2, 293–422, IV/3, 317–424; 283–357, 264–377, 274–367) That is, first Barth discusses who Christ is and what He has done for us. Then he discusses what this means for us. Between the two he inserts this transition section. What he does in these is not a transition from one locus of doctrine to another, such as from creation to reconciliation. Rather these sections are to make explicit that the move from Christ's life to Christian life is already fulfilled in Christ's existence. (IV/1, 312f.; 284)

By definition Christ's life is life with and for us. (IV/2, 294; 265f.) The event of the exaltation of the Son of man, the gift of fellowship and perfect agreement with the life of the Son of God, is Jesus' own particular history. But just because it is Jesus' particular history it is also public history, the history of the one whose life is the basis of all other men's lives. It is an event in which all participate. Jesus' history is world history; the human nature which is exalted in Him *is* our nature. We have no other. (IV/2, 298f.; 269f.)

We are what we are in Him. Our existence is "virtually accomplished" in His. (IV/2, 300; 270) In that He has kept the covenant, we have kept the covenant. In that He has obeyed God, we have obeyed God. Our existence is enclosed in His from all eternity. He has been united with God. And since this is so we are, quite prior to our subjective state, converted and obedient men. (IV/2, 299–302; 270–3) Every statement that is made about Jesus pertains also to, first, every Christian and then to every man whatsoever. (IV/2, 305; 275)

We might put it this way. In Barth's vision, that movement of God outside of himself which *is* the life history of Jesus Christ is the sole basis for the lives of all of us. We *are* only insofar as we are involved in this movement. What happens in Christ's life-history is therefore the overriding and *fundamental* part of each of our life-stories. Moreover, "history" and "being" are finally synonymous. Therefore, if Christ is good, we are good. If He is obedient, we are obedient. If His is a history of reconciliation, our histories are also stories of reconciliation and we too are reconciled men.

Clearly we strike here the nerve of Barth's system. And here we see *his* answer to the question we began with: How are we to proclaim the historical event of Jesus' existence as the meaning of all our lives? But we will return to this later. Now we must finish tracing the argument.

Thus the salvation history of all mankind occurs in Jesus' history. (IV/1, 704; 630f.) His history is the history of the reconciliation of the world with God. (IV/1, 719; 643f.)

Christ's death is our justification, not as a death instead of ours but as in the most literal sense *our* death by which *we* pass through God's judgment. His death was the death of all men independently of their attitude or behavior toward this event. It does not first become theirs in that the message about it reaches them and is heard and accepted by them, nor by virtue of the working of any churchly institutions or sacraments. No representations or applications of the Cross-event whatsoever, no canals of mediation, are needed to make it real and meaningful for them. (IV/1, 325; 295) And man's sanctification is in reality not his "own" sanctification but that which the man Jesus experienced. In His sanctification ours is included and accomplished. (IV/2, 584; 516)

This history, the history of the man Jesus with God, *is our real history.* It is much more really and directly ours than that which we see and suppose to be our history. In what we see and experience of our own lives we may very well be deceived. We may very well be watching a play of phantasms. Who knows whether his version of the events of his life bears any relation to "what really happened"? But when the Gospel tells us what has happened to us, it carries the authority of God's infallible knowledge. The history in which we are really involved with our true selves and the true selves of our fellows, with our real life-stories, is the history of our relation to God, and this is the history of Jesus Christ. (IV/1, 610f.; 547f.)

For He is the history of God with man and the history of man with God. What takes place in this history—the accusation and conviction of man as a lost sinner, his restoration, the founding and maintaining and sending of the community of God in the world, the new obedience of man—is all decided and ordained by Him as the One who primarily acts and speaks in it . . . for in Him it comes to pass that God is the reconciling God and man the reconciled man. (IV/1, 172; 158)

V

But how then can Barth speak of a history of Jesus Christ *and* His people at all? How can he speak of our "participation" in Christ's history, since His history *is* our history with God and so our whole existence? "Participation" implies that in some sense we must have life-stories distinct from that of Jesus, but has Barth left any room for this? Indeed, since for Barth man's being is his history, how can he establish any difference between Jesus and us at all? How can he speak of us participating in anything? Barth himself asks if the transition from the christological sphere to the anthropological can be anything other than establishing that the first has annulled the second. Is not a progression and a building from Jesus Christ to us excluded, excluded precisely by the completeness of what has been done for us in Jesus Christ? (IV/1, 323; 293)

Nevertheless, Barth does distinguish between our lives as they are in Christ and as "we" live them. He does not collapse Jesus and us into one undifferentiated reality. The distinction lies in the *knowledge* of what has happened in Christ. Even though our history is complete in what Jesus Christ has lived, something remains to be the distinguishing mark of our lives as *we* live them: We must come to *know* of Him and of our true lives in Him.

In all three of the transition sections the question of our participation as distinct persons in Christ's life is identical with the question of our knowledge of what has happened in Him. Christ's life is by definition life for us. But the question remains of our knowledge of what He has done on our behalf, of our knowledge of what we are in Him. It is only in this sense that there is a second step after Christology. (IV/1, 311–84; 283–348) We are what we are in Christ. But our understanding and knowledge of ourselves must become a knowledge of ourselves as those who are in Him. (IV/2, 294ff.; 265ff.). In Christ's glory as the mediator we are already included; our participation is already real. But this inclusive character of Christ's life works on us in that His Gospel reaches to those who are already the children of God but who do not yet know it. (IV/3, 321–3; 291–4) Christ's reality includes ours without swallowing it up, without abolishing us as persons, in that God *reveals* to us what has already happened to us.

So it is in the unfinished character of Christ's prophetic office, in the fact that the doing of reconciliation and perfect knowledge of it do not coincide, that there is work for "us." It is in that which remains to be done in knowing and proclaiming what He has done, that room is left for our history with God, accomplished by Christ, to be "our" history. Barth asks: Why, after God revealed himself in Christ's resurrection, are there still so many who do not know of it? And why is our knowledge of our own true selves in Christ so imperfect? Indeed, why are we still called on to believe and not allowed to see? In short, why the space in time between Easter and the Last Coming? (IV/3, 365–72; 316–22)

He answers: This delay is good because in it Christ gives us, whose reconciliation is already finished in Christ's life, time and space to participate in the fruits of reconciliation. That is, He allows the creature to take part in *proclaiming* the reconciliation which is already accomplished fact in Jesus Christ. He delays speaking the last word, He delays the trumpet at which all knees shall bow, in order to leave room for our confession and witness. (IV/3, 383f.; 331ff.) That is—and here we have the decisive formulation—Christ has not revealed himself with one stroke but has chosen to go a road from Easter to the End in order to leave room for us to exercise our freedom as reconciled creatures. (IV/3, 385f.; 333ff.) The event which constitutes "our" history, insofar as this is a realm into which the history of reconciliation progresses, is the progess of the knowledge of reconciliation in Christ. (IV/3, 419f.; 367ff.) The space between Jesus Christ's first and second coming is the space for *man's* existence. (IV/1, 367; 333)

Our history is participation in Christ's history. It is *participation*, and not a mere automatically unrolled sideshow, in that to the accomplishment of our existence in Jesus' history there is added the knowledge thereof. We exist as being distinct from Jesus in that we are those who do not fully know that we exist in Him but are *engaged in discovering this.*

The being of Jesus Christ was and is perfect and complete in itself in His history as the true Son of God and Son of Man. It does not need to be transcended or augmented by new qualities or further developments. The humiliation of God and the exaltation of man as they took place in Him are the completed fulfillment of the covenant, the completed reconciliation of the world with God. His being as such (if we may be permitted this abstraction for a moment) was and is the end of the old and the beginning of the new form of this world, even without his resurrection and ascension. He did not and does not lack anything in Himself. What was lacking was only the men to see and hear it as the work and Word of God. . . . (IV/2, 148; 132f.)

VI

Here we must be warned. It will not do to say that what happens in our lives is "merely" the progressive knowing of what happened in Christ.[11] For Christ's own life involves essentially that it shall become known.

[11] Once again we come to the central role of "knowledge" in Barth's system. Now is perhaps the place to repeat in a more general way my contention that his critics have made things too easy for themselves in saying that for Barth Christian life, etc. are "only" knowledge of eternal reality. This is no real criticism until they show *why* this "only" indicates a fault. For if we de not ignore the full connections of Barth's thought, this is not so obvious as it first appears. The most comprehensive attack is Wingren's.

In *Theology in Conflict,* pp. 23–44, 108–28, Wingren asserts: The primary contrast for Barth is not between the loving God and the rebellious creature but between God, who is for man, and the creature who because he is a creature does not know this. The central category is not God's victorious struggle to liberate his creature but revelation, understood as the mediation of knowledge. The creaturely side of the salvation event becomes a mere knowing. And the motif of struggle, so central to the biblical witness, disappears; there is no real enemy of God and man, no devil, to be seen.

Barth replies in volume IV/3 of the *Church Dogmatics.* In this volume he has located the entire creaturely historicity of the work of reconciliation in Christ's *prophetic* office. So it is quite true that the history in which God's conflict with evil takes place among us is "only" a matter of knowledge. But this "only" becomes therewith a two-edged weapon. One may say: "See how minor God's work in *our* history is; it is only the spread of knowledge of the eternal event." But one must also say: "See how great a matter Christian faith is; it is the heart of all human history and of God's work in that history."

Therefore Barth justly protests against the devaluation of the concept of knowledge, against speaking of "mere" knowledge. Christian knowledge is not a mere "knowing"; it is an event which takes place in the power of and on the basis of its object. In it Christ's work of reconciliation *occurs,* secondarily but really. Knowledge is not a merely intellectual act; it is a transformation of the entire person. (IV/3, 249–52; 118–20). It is true that we are reconciled prior to our knowledge thereof. But this statement is not to be made without reference *to* our knowledge; insofar as Barth hopes a man will be saved he hopes that he will come to the knowledge of Christ. (IV/3, 549–51; 447f.)

And although evil may be a delusion and the devil the original myth this "nihility" is the very real object of Christ's victory and a power which can ruin human life. (IV/3, 299–301; 260f.)

We must remember: God's being *ad extra* is the "proclamation of the decision in which in Himself He is who He is." (II/2, 192; 175) And man's whole being *is* his answer to God. "Man *is* in the context . . . of the process of knowing. . . ." (III/2, 211; 177) (This is my translation. The published translation of this sentence is incorrect.) "Revelation" and "knowledge" make up the concept of all extra-divine reality.

We remember from Chapter 2: God chose Jesus Christ as a creature. In doing so He chose the creature-as-such as well, the being who is not God, the being who Jesus Christ would not be by Himself. The existence of this creature-as-such is thus necessary to Christ's full reality as God's movement to a reality outside of Himself, to Christ's reality as the chosen *creature.* We say exactly the same thing in other terms when we say that we are those who are there in order to learn of their existence in Christ, and that the existence of such knowers is essential to Christ's own reality.

God chose, we said, Jesus Christ as the risen One, as man raised from the fall. And so He chose the fallen man, the man who Jesus *by himself* would not have been. He chose the mere creature, who is helpless before his own nothingness. But God chose this helpless creature only *in* the one creature who is *raised* from the fall. He has chosen *the* man, redeemed from the fall. In this man, we are fallen in ourselves and redeemed in Jesus. As this man, Jesus is fallen in us and redeemed in Himself. The one great actual reality is the reality of the creature

---

It is true that so long as the distinction between a fact and knowing it is maintained (and Barth is vehement that it must be) Barth's location of the creaturely historicity of reconciliation in the knowledge of the event of reconciliation determines the relation between our history and the event of salvation in a unique and possibly false manner. But criticism misses the mark as long as it merely notes the centrality of the contrast between knowledge and ignorance in Barth's pattern of thinking and deduces a "Barth" from there. We must not only note this schema of thought but also seek the concrete content which the concepts of knowledge and ignorance derive from the *theological* content which Barth uses them to carry. Only then will we criticize Barth instead of a caricature of him.

"If we are to discover the critical point in Barth's theology, we must concentrate our attention on the essential structure, the framework itself. If we simply note what Barth says within this framework, we miss that which is typical in his theology." (*Theology in Conflict,* p. 30) That is quite correct. But to absolutize the frame and ignore the content is even worse and prevents understanding even the frame.

who has received help, the one reality of Jesus and His people. *Within* this reality there is the dialectical determinant whereby the creature *might* not have received help; this is the *possible* existence of the creature-by-himself. Our separateness from Jesus is posited by this determinant. We exist as distinct from Jesus precisely as we, within the reality of God's union with us, His creatures, are those who might have been the creature-by-himself. We say exactly the same thing when we say: We are those who exist only in Jesus but do not yet fully realize it. (II/2, 215; 195)

Thus Christ and mankind form a whole, one person. (IV/3, 321; 278) "There is no Jesus existing exclusively for himself and there is no sinful man who is not affected and determined . . . by his existence. . . ." (IV/2, 311; 281) Man by himself is an abstraction. (Sin is the attempt to make a reality of this abstraction!) Man is Jesus Christ and His people. (IV/1, 45; 43f.) Barth can even say of Jesus Christ that "His own incarnation was completed only with the bringing of these others and their reception into the Church." (III/1, 367; 321) Jesus Christ "*is* only as *we* also are elected and called in Him." (IV/2, 334; 300) Jesus Christ is Jesus Christ and His people.

Conclusion

Jesus Christ as God and man is the one great history of the eternal covenant between God and man. Creation and reconciliation are the two sides of the actuality of this covenant, in which it occurs and is revealed.

What is the reality to which theology testifies? Other than the eternal life of God in himself? It is the one great event of the unification of God and man in Jesus Christ. At the center of this occurrence is the person of Jesus Christ himself. Surrounding Him are—in no way accidental but determined in and by the nature of the Center—the ever more widely reaching circles of the knowledge of this person.

Classical theology, we said, displayed the decisive nature of Jesus' life by describing its unique relation to the eternal realities within which all life moved and had its meaning. For a theology operating within the ancient world view eternal Being and its aspects of truth, beauty, and goodness tie the history of salvation and our own histories together; because we *are,* because we have being, we are related to these eternities; Jesus Christ is their incarnation, the place where a positive relation to them is granted us.

To put it somewhat crudely, Barth has solved the problem of the disappearance of the timeless by retaining the general structure of classical theology but putting the historical event of Jesus' existence in the place formerly occupied by changeless "Being." The eternal occurrence of Jesus Christ's life is the basis of all life. It then reveals itself especially in Jesus' own life. Thus it joins Him and us together. Or better, there is no need for us to be "bound together," no need for a middle link, for Barth proclaims the historical event itself as "Being," as the eternal basis of all life.

Thus where "is" stood there now stands "becomes." Where "Being" stood there now stands Jesus Christ. Where "Beauty," "Goodness," "Truth" in the abstract stood there now stands the life-history of Jesus. To be is to become, to become a brother of Jesus Christ, to share in His story.

CHAPTER FIVE

PREDESTINATION

In the three previous chapters the eternal "decree" or "choice" of God has been a continually recurrent theme. We have found it impossible to discuss any of the three problems without constant reference to "predestination." This is not surprising. Our topic is God's control of history. This is what is meant by "predestination,"[1] We will therefore conclude the presentation of Barth's thought with a more explicit discussion of his highly original doctrine of election. This can be very brief, yet we will see that all the strands we have been following join at this point.

Barth has made this task easy for us. For although he devotes an astonishing 563 pages of the *Church Dogmatics* to election, he begins with a section in which he lays down the structure and basic themes of the entire discussion. (II/2, #32) We will simply summarize this section.

The theme-statement which Barth puts at the head of this section reads:

The doctrine of election is the sum of the Gospel because of all words that can be said or heard it is the best: that God elects man; that God is for man too the One who loves in freedom. It is grounded in the knowledge of Jesus Christ because He is both the electing God and the elected man in One. It is part of the doctrine of God because originally God's election of man is a predestination not merely of man but of Himself. Its function is to bear basic

[1]To Barth's doctrine of predestination in general see: Balthasar, pp. 186–204; Berkouwer, pp. 76–108; Buess, *Zur Praedestinationslehre Karl Barths;* Gloege, *Zur Praedestinationslehre Karl Barths;* Kreck, *Die Lehre von der Praedestination;* Küng, pp. 29–33; Mezger, *Gottes Gnadenwahl;* Reid, *The Office of Christ in Predestination.*

testimony to eternal, free and unchanging grace as the beginning of all the ways and works of God. (II/2, 1; 3)

This statement falls into three parts: The first assertion, that the doctrine of election when rightly taught is the summary of the Gospel, is the chief motivation of all that Barth has to say on the subject. The term "election of grace" names a particular conduct of God. It is that self-determination in which He turns to man, or rather, in which He condescends to man. It is "love in the form of the deepest condescension." (II/2, 8; 10) This condescension to man is God's supreme good deed; it is the "election of *grace*." Therefore the proclamation of this basic decision of God is Gospel, good news. But it is Gospel not only because it is grace but also because it is election; "the *election* of grace" is Gospel. That grace is God's completely free act of choice means that it is not caused or motivated by anything other than itself. Therefore there is nothing that can undo it, nothing that can call it into question. When God's election of grace is proclaimed to me the grace which it contains is absolutely dependable. Therefore it is Gospel. (II/2, 7–11; 9–12)

Since the doctrine of election is the sum of the Gospel, it must testify to an *affirmative* choice by God. It must witness to a decision of God about us which is God's acceptance and adoption of us. If God's decision were "Yes" *and* "No," then everything would remain uncertain. To be told that my life hung from this decision would be anything but good news. One must not make election and reprobation equal partners. One must not make them two equal varieties of God's choice; rather one must always speak of acceptance and rejection in such a way that acceptance is always the real content of God's decision. (II/2, 13–5; 13–6)

Barth is concerned above all to make clear that the proclamation of God's election is a concentrated version of the good news of the Gospel. He is concerned to make clear that it is news, and so a message about what *God* has done, a message about His freedom. He is concerned to make clear that it is good, and so a message of love, of light with no darkness at all. His entire luxurious development of the doctrine of election follows from this. The proclamation of predestination is the last sharpening of the Gospel; in it the last certainty about God's intent for us is abolished.

This brings us to the second part of the theme-statement. In order to be the summary of the Gospel, the doctrine of election must be doctrine about Jesus Christ. For He is the content of the Gospel. It must be a doctrine about Jesus Christ and so not about a dark and obscure "absolute decree," not about the mysterious decisions of a distant and unknown deity.

What can be the basis of this doctrine? It can be neither tradition, nor pastoral utility, nor the experience that some seem to be saved and others not, nor a deduction from the doctrine of God's omnipotence. All such approaches to the doctrine of election deal with God-in-general and man-in-general. But this is neither the God nor the man of whom Scripture speaks. (II/2, 37ff.; 35ff.)

The God of Scripture, and so the God of the Christian doctrine of election, is the God who works in the history of His people. He is not the hidden God who dwells in abstract eternity, but the God at work in our lives. This means, finally, that He is the God who is at work in the history of Jesus Christ. Here is where God's decree is fulfilled. Therefore here is where we must look to find the subject of the act of election. In order to see the God who elects we must look to Jesus Christ. (II/2, 55–8; 51–4)

Accordingly, the man whom God chooses, the man of Scripture, is never everybody in general and nobody in particular. He is always a particular man; He is Abraham, Israel, Moses. Finally he is *the* particular man, Jesus Christ. The elect man is Jesus Christ. To see the object of election we must look to Jesus Christ. (II/2, 58–62; 55–8)

Jesus Christ is therefore the basis of the doctrine of election. All its statements must be statements about Him. In Him we see the God who elects. In Him we see the man who is chosen. And in Him these two come together; i.e. in Him election takes place. The knowledge of election is simply a particular form of the knowledge of Christ. (II/2, 62ff.; 58ff.)

There is no other God of election behind God-in-Jesus Christ. Therefore the old Calvinist doctrine which called Christ the mirror of election is not adequate. For if God's original decision about us is distinct from what happens in Jesus Christ, if it is only *mirrored* in Jesus Christ, then this decision and not what is decided in Christ will be decisive. Our relation to God will not in the last analysis be a relation in and through Christ. And the mirror will be impossible to trust completely. Nor does the old Lutheran doctrine of God's universal good will to all men help. It is much too general to give comfort in the actual crises of life. Jesus Christ himself must take the place of all such hidden decrees and highest axioms. Only then will our knowledge of salvation be certain, only then will talk of God's eternal decision be Gospel. (II/2, 64ff., 81f.; 60ff., 75f.)

And now the third part of the theme-statement. The Gospel of election is Gospel *in that* it shows that grace is the beginning and deepest reality of all that God does. The doctrine of election is part of the doctrine of God, of the doctrine about the subject of God's works. It does not only appear when we come to speak of what God does; it is the presupposition of all that

God does; it is part of the description of the person who does them.

The decision in which God is God, in which He decides who and what He shall be, is precisely this decision to accept man. God's being is love and freedom; election is the act in which He exercises this love and freedom. It is the actual reality of love and freedom—and so of God himself. God *is* the one who elects man. Therefore we must describe election as an event in God's life as He lives it in and of Himself. It is in this act of choosing man that God is the eternally living God. Barth uses the expression *opus dei internum ad extra:* Election is an interior act of God like the eternal love of the Father for the Son and of the Son for the Father, but it is that particular internal act in which He relates Himself to a reality other than Himself. It is in this act that He is the Triune God and not otherwise. He could have been the living Triune God in some other act, but in fact is not. The doctrine of election is the description of the decision in which God is God. (II/2, 82–6; 76–80)

Thus the word which stands at the beginning of all Christian words is the doctrine of reconciliation, of the salvation of sinners. Before God does any of His works He is the reconciler. God's decision to reconcile sinful man is the presupposition of all His works. (II/2, 96; 89) God's work outside himself is one great uninterrupted act of rule, proceeding from His decision to reconcile sinful man to Himself in Jesus Christ. (II/2, 97; 90)

It is in this dignity that the doctrine of election has its function, that it shows grace to be the beginning of all the works and ways of God. (II/2, 99; 91f.)

CHAPTER SIX

REFLECTIONS

Yea and Amen

"And God be praised, today a theology has again been given us which 'teaches rightly of grace.' " (Eduard Thurneysen, farewell sermon in the Minster, Basel, June 21, 1959.) It is time to ask: What shall we say of all this? It will already be clear that the writer cannot agree with everything. Indeed I must object at some points which are perhaps the dearest to Karl Barth himself, which are systematic hinges of his thought. Yet before everything else there must be added a quiet Amen to Eduard Thurneysen's tribute to his old friend. Here is indeed a theology which teaches of grace. And also those of us for whom Barth has not become the only master and teacher must join in thanking for this gift. There is too much theology which does not teach grace to do otherwise. Beset by the resurgence of an "evangelical" conversion of the Gospel into an ideology tailored to our terror of the present and by our chronic retreat to churchmanship, ideals, and psychology, we need to listen carefully to this joyful proclamation of grace in Christ. More, we must join in thanking for a theology which teaches "rightly" of grace, for in that sense of the word which matters before the Lord of theology, if it teaches His grace, it teaches it rightly.

As we rather hopelessly turn to preaching, to the attempt to say something to people at once skeptical and superstitious, to people bereft of a framework of inherited certainties, to people bereft of the values to which it has been so convenient to appeal, Barth reminds us that we should speak directly and simply to our hearers as they and we are. There is no need to embark on the endless preliminary of first persuading men to return to the convictions of their fathers, so that next we may show them how they fail to measure up to these convictions, so that finally we may speak of God's mercy. We can speak without needing to appeal to these now shaky bridges between Christ and ourselves.

We need no bridges at all between Christ and ourselves, these or any other. Our relation to God's revelation of himself in His Son is not something apart from our ordinary lives as human doers and sufferers. It is not something which comes second, so that we are first involved in our history and the history of our world—and then faced with the choice of whether also to become involved with God's Word. The message of the Church does not need to create a point of contact with human life. The Word *is* that "other" over against whom human life is lived.[1]

Barth has shown us how this fact may be described theologically, how we may provide a theology for proclamation to the nihilists. Our inherited theology, whether "liberal" or "conservative" has operated by first developing an understanding of what human life is and of what the world we live in is. After having done this it has then inquired as to how Christ might have altered or confirmed this structure. Whether this previously given understanding of existence was derived from experience, speculation, or the Bible is unimportant; it came first and Christ was fitted in afterwards. Barth has turned this schema on its head. He proclaims Christ as the goal of all that happens and the shaper of all reality.

He has shown how, if only we take the Gospel about the God

[1] I hope that the whole point of departure for this study will prevent anyone from supposing that I am advocating a "Barthian" approach where this Gospel is preached at the heads of the hearers without concern for its contact with their actual self-understanding—any more than Barth does.

who *does* things with full seriousness, if only we allow our conceptions of "God" and "man" and "being" to be shaped by it, the gulf between Christ and ourselves is discovered to be illusory.[2] Moreover, his christological ontology does this without the naïveté of so much "biblical" event-theology. God *is* God-revealing-himself, not secondarily but primarily. Man *is* the one called into self-transcendence by God's presence. Once we begin to understand this we begin also to see how Jesus Christ can be exhibited in His unadulteratedly temporal reality as the meaning of men's lives. God *occurs.* He occurs in the life of Jesus Christ. And we *occur* as God thus gives us himself as that "other" without whom historical life is impossible.

Turning to the more particular positions described in this study, this "Amen" must take the form of recognizing that Barth has insights which are decisive and behind which it would be foolish to retreat. If it be true that the last secret of God is proclaimed in the Gospel of Christ, that we who have heard this Gospel need not be in any way uncertain about His intentions for us, then it follows that we must agree with Barth on the following points.

We must agree in rejecting the commonsense view that the Incarnation was God's second choice in view of the failure of an original plan for a natural perfecting of creation. Quite probably the deeply unchristian slogan which passes universally for piousness: "I'll do the best I can and God will forgive the rest," has its roots in just the separation of creation and reconciliation which Barth rejects. We must learn to see God's grace in Christ as the point from which we live, not as an emergency help for those occasions when our own moral endeavors prove inadequate.

[2] Barth laughs at Lessing's "great gulf" as a pseudo-problem.

We must learn that our good deeds and our bad deeds alike are meaningful and useful only because of God's grace.

Accordingly, we will not attack the definition of creation as the "outer basis" of the covenant. We might wish to use different terminology. But creation must indeed be understood on the basis of the purposes of God's love, purposes which go beyond all that is given in creation and all that would of itself grow out of creation.

It is also true that the only covenant that exists is the broken and restored covenant, the covenant of reconciliation, the covenant with sinners. It is true that nothing permits us to invent a covenant in general and to propose this as the original object of God's plan. The purpose of creation is not opened up by speculation about what would have happened if man had not sinned. Creation can only be believed when we see it from what actually happened in Christ, from Calvary. Therefore it is right to describe creation as a victory of God. It is right to see God's continuing rule of His creation as standing in the service of His saving grace.

Even Barth's controversial doctrine of evil cannot be rejected out of hand. If evil "exists" at all it must somehow have a place in God's will. Without flat contradiction of the whole Christian witness, this place can only be God's rejection. As Barth justly remarks: "It is not speculation, but a description which even the veriest child can understand, simply to say of evil in the first instance that it is what God does not will." (IV/3, 202; 177) To be sure, Barth's statement that evil is that which is rejected by God is rather more than such a simple description. It is intended as a definition. But if meaningful statements are to be made about evil, such as "God has overcome evil in

Christ," we must have some conception of what it is. This must certainly be: Evil is that which is what it is in that God rejects it. And if we are not to deny the existence of evil altogether, we must also say: Evil exists exactly in that God rejects it.

Having come so far, we must continue with Barth and reject the view that reconciliation is only God's reaction to sin. If God's will to rescue and exalt us in Christ is really to be God's last secret, then it must be His eternal will as He is eternal. It cannot be merely His reaction to anything. The coming of Jesus Christ to sinful man is, as Barth says, its own sufficient reason.

This brings us to the subject matter of Chapter 3. Here too there is much to affirm. I believe Barth is correct in abolishing the division between a God throned in abstract eternity, who there "decides" what is to occur in time, and a God-in-Christ who in time carries these plans out. If what happened in Christ is really God's will for us, if it is not secondary to a prior, abstract, and largely unknown will of God, then it indeed follows that God's decision to be merciful falls not "above" but *in* the life of Jesus Christ. His life is this decision.

If this is so, if the God who rules history is the active God, the God who is the chief Person of history, if He is Jesus Christ, then the line between the Son "before" the Incarnation and the Incarnate Son cannot be so neatly drawn as is often presupposed. Then it will not do to see the life of the God-man as merely one in the series of temporal events—not even when it is regarded as the event which is the goal or "midpoint" of all the others. Barth is right in regarding the life of Jesus Christ as an *eternal* event, as the transcendent presupposition and basis of all other happenings. In Him, the eternal happens.

Continuing with the subject matter of Chapter 3, the doctrine that the covenant is the "inner basis" of the creation is also to be accepted. It is not prying into God's secrets to ask what His motive in creating us was. It is simply obedience to Jesus Christ. And it is also only obedience to God's self-revelation to say that it was God's love for His Son and for those who would share His Son's humanity that moved Him to create them.

After all this, it must be obvious that the critique which follows is not intended as an assault. I am far too convinced of the necessity of Barth's thought and too impresed by what is to be learned from him. Yet I am also convinced that there are aspects of our situation as hearers of God's Word which somehow remain invisible to Barth.

But Woe Unto That Man by Whom the Son of Man Is Delivered

Can one, as does Karl Barth, depict the long history of God with man as a history comprehended in one great decision of God? Can one, as does Karl Barth, depict the crises and conflicts and victories, the great antinomies of judgment and grace, of wrath and love, of hiddenness and revelation which this history unrolls, as comprehended within a solution given in advance, in pretemporal eternity? The will of God is one and eternal; but is this unity that of a master plan where each step is taken "in order" to accomplish the next? Have we given the mystery of God's rule of human history, in which so much of evil and of God's wrath appears, its full weight when we say that it is all done "in order" to show mercy? Can we do this without also saying something else, something less satisfactory to our desire to have everything in its place? I doubt it. Barth's description of the will of God in Christ is in itself a major event in the history of theology. But the relation between this will and God's rule in the rest of history is rather more complicated and paradoxical than Barth will allow it to be.

I

This can be seen clearly if we analyze what is involved in confessing that God is the Creator. As God's revelation of himself in Jesus Christ first opens up our lives to us, we do not find ourselves automatically in the kingdom of God's Grace. We find ourselves eating and drinking, loving and hating. We find ourselves amidst wars and rumors of wars. And we find ourselves doing these things, acting and suffering, in the course of man's grandiose attempt to live without God. It is exactly this, that we are attempting to live without God, which is revealed to us. For we find ourselves gathered around Calvary, attempting to eliminate God once and for all from our lives.

Our life as we simply find ourselves living it, what the revelation teaches us to call "creation," first opens itself to us as the "old age," as an order of things embodying the awful double secret of our rebellion and God's wrath. This is not a sentence of philosophy, empirical observation, or natural theology; the world encounters us in this way precisely in the revelation of God in Jesus Christ. For this revelation puts us at Calvary. And here we see that when God carries out His will, He *fights* with the powers of this world. The historical and natural forces which dominate our lives are revealed as *enemies* of God, and we as willing captives.

This negative encounter with reality is not inauthentic. It is true that the revelation next teaches us to penetrate through the old age to the loving Father of Jesus Christ who is its Creator. But this does not mean that the negative encounter with reality is a delusion, or perhaps a mere stratagem on God's part. We first meet the creation in the guise of the kingdom of Satan, and this meeting is authentic, exactly as authentic as the Crucifixion. Our experience of God's creative work is complicated by the fact that the product of that work confronts us first as the old age, as reality which denies us. This complication is not to be evaded or short-circuited.

In that Jesus Christ meets us with the last word and final decision about our lives He reveals Himself as Lord also of the life we find ourselves living and over all the forces which control that life. We recognize Him not only as Savior but as Origin of our lives. We recognize the God who reveals Himself in Christ as the Creator. The knowledge of Creation is the knowledge of the absolute power and authority of the God who has reconciled us in Jesus Christ—absolute power and authority without which He could not be our Lord and Savior.

Thus faith sees the wrath of God which is the secret of the present age as a work of the God of love. It claims the angry ruler of history as the Father of Jesus Christ. It is freed to confess: "I believe that God . . . has given and still preserves to me my body and soul . . . that He daily provides abundantly for all the needs of my life . . . and that He does this purely out of fatherly and divine goodness and mercy. . . ." [3] It is freed to receive the world in which it finds itself, with all the sin and evil which mark it, as the good gift of the Father of Christ.

Thus faith sees in God's rule of wrath, under which so much is lost and so little saved, God's persistence in an original intent which has now been fulfilled in Christ's love. It therefore recognizes that this is a good intent. We and our world are, despite

[3] Luther's explanation of the first article of the Apostles' Creed.

all, God's creation and His good creation. But just because this is revealed at the *Cross* where God does *battle* against us, against our lives and our world, where He *condemns* and rejects our rebellion, where the history whose secret is sin is *contradicted* by grace, this confession of Creation is and remains a mighty "nevertheless."

It is only because of the unity of God's act of creation with His act of reconciliation that reality as we find it can be God's good creation. And this is of course just what Barth says. But this unity is highly paradoxical and indirect. When God acts to save us He also unveils our existence as His creation, but He does so just in that He *overcomes* and *triumphs* over it. The creature is the creature precisely in that God can overcome its rebellion. The world as the old age is still God's creation in that it remains entirely subject to His will, which means that it remains subject to His victory over it. Thus the unity of creation and reconcilation is an event which occurs only in the contradiction between the world and God. The confession "This world is the work of the Father of Grace," is a *victory,* both as a word which God speaks to us and as our answering confession. It is a victory which only happens in the battle between Christ and the very world which is thus named God's creation, which only happens in the real hell and damnation of the Cross.

The confession, "This world is the work of the Father of grace," is by no means obvious. It says that the Father of Jesus Christ is also the ruler of this dark history of mankind. It says precisely that the old age is a gift of His love. It says that reconciliation is not a creation out of nothing, but that the old age is the flesh in which the new age of God's love becomes incarnate—precisely as the old, evil, dark age. Everything that this sentence says, that the God of this world is the God of love, that the Creator of a world like this is the Father of Jesus, who creates good and only good, that we may know in the midst of very real catastrophes that the God of those catastrophes does everything for our sakes—everything that this sentence says stands under the sign of the "nevertheless" of the Cross. Only there is it true. Otherwise it is not only unknowable but still untrue.

Therefore the unity of creation and reconciliation consists exclusively in the personal unity of Jesus Christ. He is the Agent of Creation and He is the Reconciler. The unity of creation and reconciliation is the unity of His history as the history of one person. It is only in that it is subject to the Reconciler that this world remains God's creation. The possibility of the doctrine of creation lies solely in the unity of creation and reconciliation in the "lifework" of the Son. Nor is this unity a part of either creation or reconciliation in themselves; on the contrary these events are so related to each other that it becomes a miracle that the Son retains His personal identity as He goes through both, that His achieving of personal identity becomes death and resurrection. The unity of creation and reconciliation, the unity in which this world in which we live, and not some past state, is God's good creation for us, is the unity wrung out by Christ between Golgotha and Easter.

The unity of creation and reconciliation is the unity of one Person's history. Therefore it cannot be regarded as given in advance. His history cannot be regarded as the implementation of what is really already accomplished with the first event of that history. Rather the unity of His history is a truly historical unity, i.e. a unity which *occurs* in the succession of the deeds of which His history is composed. There was a time when He was the Agent of Creation but not yet the Reconciler. That the agent of creation *is* the Reconciler is a unity which only happens in the event in which He *becomes* the Reconciler. It is a unity given in the overcoming, in the "nevertheless" which is the history of the Crucified and Risen.

Here then is the criterion which dictates a certain caution over against Barth's development: No proposition may be made about creation and its relation to reconciliation in Christ which removes the "nevertheless" in which alone this relation is real. Barth is in some danger of doing this.[4]

We may not read the order of things established by Christ's work of reconciliation, the order of sin and forgiveness, back into God's work of creation. We may not use the message of forgiveness as a principle by which to describe the act of creation and the reality of the creature. Most particularly we may not use it as an explanation of the awful duality in which given existence opens itself to us, as an explanation of the fact that the world first meets us as a realm of wrath.

Creation makes the necessary arrangements for a covenant which is in fact a covenant with sinners. But it is not the preparation for this covenant *qua* covenant with sinners. The imperfection of creation is no doubt a shadow cast by its need of re-

[4] Regin Prenter has an objection to make at this point which will add to our discussion. (*Die Einheit von Schoepfung und Erloesung*) We summarize his argument: Creation is for and through Christ. Good, but how? According to Barth, through *analogies* which make the connection of creation to Christ visible. Indeed, these analogies *are* the connection. Faith in Christ discovers them and thus achieves insight into the secret of creation. Thus for Barth knowledge of creation is *insight* into man's determination by God, an insight made possible by faith in Christ; creation is not itself a direct object of faith, the believer *knows* and *grasps* the secret of creation. But against this position Prenter objects that the unity of creation and redemption is objective only in God; it does not become transparent for us. Barth uses Christ's death and resurrection as a *principle* with which to make the world understandable. He seeks to stand above the concrete contradictions of our world—in eternity where these analogies may well be valid—but it is not in this rarefied air that the cross of Christ is planted.

demption. And all of this is indeed comprehended in God's knowledge and will. But it is also evil without qualification. Sin, fall, suffering, the Cross, all are comprehended in the back side of God's eternal decision. But God's will and his unwill, his creating and his not-creating are neither joined nor separated as the inevitable two sides of one coin.[5]

II

Whenever the Christian message has had any depth or fullness it has declared that the coming of Jesus Christ was unconditionally necessary, that it was decreed by the Lord of all in His absolute freedom, that it was decreed by God before all time. It has declared Him and our life with Him to be the goal of all history and of God's rule of history. He came as "the times were fulfilled," His Kingdom was "prepared before the foundation of the world." His Passion is *the* hour, the hour of the End. He was delivered up by "the definite plan and foreknowledge of God." We were chosen "in him before the foundation of the world . . . according to his purpose . . . in Christ as a plan for the fulness of time." "For the Son of man goes as it is written of him. . . ."[6] ". . . But woe to that man by whom the Son of man is betrayed!" And here we arrive at the same unresolved tension that we found in the Christian confession of creation. The mystery of God's rule in the decisions and crises of nations and in the motives and obscure turnings of our lives is revealed but not dispelled by His rule in the events of salvation.

Beyond doubt, the Christian message proclaims that God has

[5] For an exegesis of the New Testament passages directly relevant to this section see my Heidelberg dissertion, pp. 223–37.

[6] For an exegesis of the relevant New Testament passages see my Heidelberg dissertion, pp. 262–77, 283–85.

absolutely and eternally decided to reconcile sinful man by sending His son to be ours. Beyond doubt, it also proclaims that He as the Creator directs all history to this goal. But the relation between these two predestinings is not without qualification to be described as an identity. In order that *all* may receive grace, the Son of man must go as has been decreed—but woe to that man through whose agency this is accomplished. It is love and mercy only which motivates and is the coming of Christ. But the divine rule which serves that decision and leads to that coming is and remains double predestination, a rule of God in which His wrath is present and active.

It cannot be too drastically asserted that God commands all things to the end that man shall be saved through Christ. But this direction of history and of God's will is hidden by man's rebellion and God's judgment—and this hiddenness is more than ignorance. The Gospel does not *explain* the rule of history's hidden Lord.

God has eternally decided to create us. He has eternally decided to transcend creation and make of us sons led by His Son. He has eternally decided to reconcile fallen man to Himself through the suffering Incarnation of His Son. These decisions are all one in the one God. But the way in which Barth displays this unity is not prefigured by the Gospel. The Gospel of forgiveness does not establish the unity of God's will through a series of "in order thats."

Our salvation lies in a decision of God, the decision by which Jesus Christ lives as God for us. Karl Barth's understanding of this decision is in all essentials correct: It is its own basis. It carries its eternal validity within itself. So far as this decision in and of itself is concerned even Barth's "supralapsarianism" is correct: God's love for sinners in Christ is not merely His accommodation to an unfortunate situation but the opening of a depth in God in which He loves and sacrifices himself for the sinner as sinner. Grace is not a repair job. It *is* God's will and the basis of our whole existence.

When this decision is carried out on us, another will of God is opened up to us. This is His will to create us, to create us as creatures destined to transcend ourselves and participate in His life. It is His will to preserve and rule us for this goal. But because this will of God becomes visible in reconciliation, in forgiveness, it appears to us as the judgment which it becomes to the creature who rejects it. It appears as God's attack on our created lives, as His closing of the way to participation in His life. It appears as that rule of God in nature and history which carries the double secret of man's rebellion and God's rejection.

These two decisions are revealed as decisions of one God. Indeed, God's mysterious rule of nature and history is revealed as serving His love in Christ. But it serves it at the Cross, there where God makes the apex of our sin and His judgment into His unfathomable acceptance. It serves it at the Cross, and so as the judgment, the refusal of grace, which in itself it is.

The "pre-" in "predestination" is God's declaration that what He does in Christ is His absolute will for us. It declares the identity of the Father of Jesus Christ with the Creator and ruler of history. It declares that we may trust the decision which falls in Christ, that it is not compromised by some other will of God, that the fearsome rule of history's Lord stands to serve it. It declares the final validity of the will of God in Christ by revealing that the God who there reveals Himself is the same God who has done all that went before, and that He has now brought it about that all that went before leads to this. But it does not deny, it affirms and insists, that something did go before, that something different, something fearsome went before. The "pre-" in "predestination" affirms the finality of God's will in Christ by revealing it to be the will of the God who works all things. It does this precisely by affirming the reality of the wrath which occurs in this working. In His sole power as Creator, God moves all things to His will in Christ. But within His rule of the world this appears as double predestination, as forgiveness *and* condemnation.

"The Son of man goes as is written of him, but woe to that man by whom the Son of man is betrayed! . . ."

What I have done with these suggestions is to dissolve the "in order that" with which supralapsarianism old and new ties together the elements of God's will and works. Does this then produce an "infralapsarian" position? And so postulate an undefined, eminently religious will of God-in-the-abstract? That is, have I gone back to the position which Barth overcame? No. For that will of God which we have described as "not yet," his decision to send Christ, is in no sense abstract. It is not at all hidden in the sense of "unknown." It is absolutely concrete and defined. It is the will not of God-in-general, but of the God to whom Christ cried: "My God, my God, why hast thou forsaken me?"

Then have I—worse yet—postulated an independent realm of God's wrath? Have I neatly divided reality into two kingdoms, one ruled by a "God" indistinguishable from an angry demon? Not at all. The reality with which we have to do is the history of God and man, and there is but one such history. But it does not follow that this history contains but one event. God's condemnation serves His grace. Only it does not serve it by becoming itself grace, but in the mode of suffering and overcoming.

It serves it in the conflict which God takes upon himself in the course of His history with rebellious mankind.

Christ the Will of God

What then *is* the nature of the unity of God's will and work, if it is not constituted by a series of "in order thats"? All God's works are one in Jesus Christ. But what does this mean if it does not mean quite what Barth says it does?

I

Whenever the Christian Gospel is expounded with particular attention to the question of God's presence to us and our knowledge of Him a *movement* takes place. God moves out of eternity into time, out of distance into nearness, out of timelessness into history. The gods of religion are all abstract and timeless, even the offensively naturalistic. The Gospel relocates God; it says: The Life you seek—it is Jesus! The Bread you seek—it is Jesus! It is the words you now hear and the food you now eat! [7]

The most striking and true side of Barth's doctrine of God's rule of history is his insistence that the act of will by which God rules is identical with the history of Jesus Christ. God's grace does not float above Christ; Christ *is* God's grace. Jesus Christ *is* God ruling human history, for the goal of our rescue and glory.

But a moment's thought discovers that such an identification of God's eternal will and the history of Jesus can mean one of two things. It might mean that the will and decree of God comes into our history to dwell among us. But it might also

[7] For an exegesis of the relevant Johannine texts see my Heidelberg dissertation, pp. 258–60.

mean that the basic content of Jesus' life leaves our history to occupy that place in the heavens previously held by the predestinating God of old Calvinism. The first would be consonant with the movement of the Gospel, the second would not. In which direction does the identification of God's will and Jesus' history move in Karl Barth's thought?

It does not seem possible to avoid suspecting that for him the movement *tends* in the false direction. Where for the Gospel God's will and rule becomes Jesus Christ, it is to be feared that for Barth Jesus Christ has become the eternal decree.[8]

The dangerous point is Barth's use of the concepts of analogy and knowledge to describe temporal history. He distinguishes very explicitly between God's eternal history and temporal history including the history of Jesus of Nazareth. Temporal history is the *knowledge* of reconciliation and so the *knowledge* of what happens in Christ, of His essential history. The *fact* of reconciliation and so the essential history of Jesus Christ is therewith correlated to eternal history.

Jesus Christ is the eternal decree of God before all time. Jesus Christ is the history in Palestine which reveals this decree. Barth does not separate these two; his concept of revelation and knowledge is far too rich. But we must still ask: Which is the prior definition? Barth defines the history in time as the revelation

[8] This objection must be distinguished from that of Bouillard: "But since, according to him, faith and obedience have only to attest an act to which they have nothing to contribute, the history of salvation appears to be a divine drama which is played far above man. One may reiterate that all this concerns and includes us; the words seem to float above us—a christological dream projected on a platonic heaven." (vol. 3, p. 291) See also vol. 2, pp. 73–107; vol. 3, p. 292.

By the "human history" which Bouillard fears that Barth renders irrelevant Bouillard understands our *activity*. When I say something very similar I mean by human history the encounters in which we, within given existence, come to transcend the given for the not yet given. Who is active in such an encounter depends entirely on who encounters whom.

and analogy of eternal history and so gives his answer. And with this answer he puts himself in danger of removing reconciliation itself, the inner reality of Jesus' life, from our history.

There is no objection to making the concept of knowledge the key for a description of the temporal event of salvation. The Gospel of John does just that. But when John makes revelation the essence of the temporal history of Christ, then revelation is not revelation *of* God's history with man, revelation *is* God's history with man. What is revealed is not the unity of God and man, it is simply God—and the revelation is itself the unity with Him.

There is at least the possibility that what has happened in Barth's christological interpretation of God's will and rule is, exactly as he says: that "Jesus Christ himself . . . occupies this place" (the place of the absolute decree of Calvinism) (II/2, 81; 75)—all too literally. This movement would oppose both the movement of the Gospel and the need of present theology. Rather we must seek to describe God's will—its eternity undiminished—as an event in history, as the chronologically and geographically fixable event of the life of Jesus of Nazareth, the Christ. We wish to speak of God's decision and, in so doing, speak more unequivocally than Barth of the life of Jesus Christ in our history, of His life in created time and space. Jesus Christ is God's great decision about us, and not as an event in a "third" level between time and eternity. In *our* history God makes His *eternal* decision.

II

If we thus fix our attention on temporal history we see how to understand the unity of God's decisions and works without collapsing them into one and without dividing them. The unity of wrath and mercy in God's work, the unity of his decrees, the unity of the Crucifixion with the Resurrection, is an *historical* unity.[9]

The unity of history (supposing there to be any such thing) is not given in advance. History is newness, self-transcendence. It does not simply unroll from an all-determining origin. Nor does it have a goal built into its progress so as to be immanently ruled by its goal. Certainly there is necessity also in history; if we can speak of God ruling it there must be. But the necessary connection of each event with the past is established when it occurs and by its occurring and not before. The pattern of history in which each event has its necessary place and meaning, in which we may find a unity of events, *is itself a happening.*

We must be very careful in speaking of "God's decree" in the singular. We must be very careful not to draw hard lines between God's deciding "in eternity" and God's ever new decrees in the history of His people. Throughout His history with fallen man, God has chosen. He chose the patriarchs, He chose Israel out of Egypt, He chose David. When we confess this choosing of God we do not turn to a history other than that one which has occurred in our time and space. We turn directly to it. He chose to condemn sinful man and He chose to rescue and exalt him. He chose the Crucifixion and He chose the Resurrection.

God's "two" decisions stand in that relation of identity in difference which we discussed in the previous section in that God's decision of mercy in Christ *follows* His decision of judgment. They are two steps in one history. Thus neither can be

[9] For an exegesis of the New Testament passages see my Heidelberg dissertation, pp. 262–77.

defined by the other, or predicted from the other, or subsumed under the other; yet they are one.

God's will is one and eternal. But the oneness of God's eternal will is nevertheless not given from all eternity but is achieved by God within temporal history. It is constituted in the succession of God's decisions, in particular in the succession of the Crucifixion and Resurrection. It is an eternal unity achieved in time. The unity of God's one eternal will is an event which occurred in time at the Cross. It is this one drastic sentence which separates us from Barth. Where he puts an "in order that," there should stand the Cross.

The unity of God's will is a unity which He has won through conflict and victory. That God condemns *and* saves without self-contradiction, that He condemns in order to save, this is something which He has accomplished in His history in this world with men. And that not without cost.

III

Turning to the christological ontology of all this, it is true that God does *all* his works through the one Person who is the God-man, Jesus Christ. But the unity of the Son's life is the unity of a *life*. It is, therefore, a unity which at each moment of decision must be established afresh. The ontological unity of God's work is the despair and triumph of Good Friday and Easter. It is the unity of the life of that One who as the Crucified was not yet the Risen until He *became* the one eternal Crucified and Risen.

Are all things created in the God-*man* Jesus Christ? Surely we must say: The Son *is* the God-man. And if we were correct in agreeing that the Incarnation is its own eternal basis, then this "is" is eternally valid. It would be easy to conclude that the God-man was as such the Agent of creation—and Barth does. Moreover, Barth rightly refuses to speak of the Incarnation in abstraction from sin and our need of rescue. The further conclusion seems inevitable that salvation from sin is the basis of creation—and Barth draws it. Yet somehow this train of conclusions seems to lead to a false position. Again, there was a time when the Agent of creation was not yet the Reconciler, until He *became* the eternal Reconciler.

We cannot dispense with the concept of the *logos asarkos,* of a life and work of the Son *before* his union with man. To be sure, we cannot draw the line in the simple way: The not yet incarnate Son is eternal, then He puts on human reality. For if the Incarnation is an eternal decision, if it is its own eternal presupposition, we must indeed speak of an eternity of the God-man. Yet if the Incarnation is not the one and only event in the history of God with man, if somehow we must speak of "two" decisions and works of God, then we must be wary of calling this eternity a *pre*existence of the God-man. Then there is a work and decision of God which can only be related to Christ through the concept of the eternal Son. Then there is a work of God the Christology of which can only be expressed by the concept of the not yet incarnate Word.

For this concept brings to expression the fact that God's work and decision in the human life of Christ *follows* another work, which is not directly identical with it. God always works in and through His Son who is Jesus Christ; but this work was not always the work of reconciliation. We must therefore speak of a preexistence of Christ as the *logos asarkos,* in strict correspondence to the Creator's mysterious work of judgment, to the rule of the hidden Lord of history.[10] The God who reveals himself in Christ is the Lord of all things. But His rule often cannot be understood directly from His grace in Christ; He is the same God but God in a different way. It is this indirectness which the concept of the Son who has not yet put on flesh brings to expression.

The vision of the Incarnate Son as eternal and that of the Son before His Incarnation are both necessary to grasp the immense claim that all God's works among us are done in Christ. We have to do with stages in the life of the one Person who is Jesus Christ. Further harmonization does not seem possible.

Inclusive Christology

Finally, that great central vision which comprehends all reality in Christ's history as God and man is inevitably touched by these criticisms. If God's decrees and acts cannot be comprehended as one save through the course of human history, this touches the shape of Barth's construction. And our objection to Barth's use of the analogy concept, if correct, impugns the mortar. Nor is it obvious that Christ's history can stand being regarded as "principle and essence" of all happenings whatsoever. Is there not something abstract about "principle" and "essence"? Is there not a danger that in Barth's hands Christ's history threatens to

[10] See Emil Brunner, *Dogmatic,* vol. 1, pp. 230–4. But I would *not* say as he has said: "The mystery of God is not exhausted by the Son; for '*pater est fons totius trinitatis*'; God *can* be other than the One revealed in Jesus Christ as Light and Life, namely, the Hidden God, who as such operates not in the Word and its light, but in that which is not 'word'. . . in darkness." (p. 230)

Barth sees the connection between the *deus absconditus* and the *logos asarkos* very decisively—and precisely for this reason rejects the latter concept.

turn into something mightily resembling a metaphysical idea? Despite Barth's intent and protestations?

Yet the magnificent force and coherence which this vision gives to Barth's proclamation of Christ cannot be abandoned without a struggle. This is not the place to attempt to develop a full theological ontology which will take both Barth's achievement and our criticisms seriously. I only want to indicate one relevant line of thought.

For Barth, God's history with man is the history of God and man "in" the person of Jesus Christ. In Chapter 3 we contrasted this with another possibility. Might it not be that the history of God with man in Jesus Christ is not in the first place God's history with man-in-Christ but the history of God-in-Christ with mankind? Might it not be that the starting point is not what God does *to* Jesus but what He does *through* Jesus? Might it not be that Jesus' history indeed creates and determines all history, but less as the history which *includes* all history than as the history which *makes* all history? [11]

Back to the Beginning

I

What is God's goal for His creatures? Barth answers: The life of Jesus Christ, as God's life with and for unworthy man, is the

[11] What I propose is to attempt to realize in this particular area the motive which lay behind the classical Lutheran doctrine of the *communicatio idiomatum, genus maiestaticum.*

Barth himself has given a fine definition of the motivation of the old Lutheran dogmaticians: "Their concern was that the divine triumph over the distinction and antithesis between God and man took place directly, and is a fact, in the humanity of Jesus Christ." (IV/2, 71; 66)

only goal of history. The eternal will of God is His will that this life shall take place. All else is willed as the means to this end. We could not wish a more unequivocal answer to the first of the three questions we untangled from our "introductory cliché." Moreover, once someone has said it this flatly, it seems odd that Christian theology could ever have hesitated over other answers or no answer at all.

Yet perhaps there were good reasons for that hesitation. God's very revelation of the goal of life in fellowship with Jesus Christ impresses on believers a sense of discontinuity between their lives and that goal. Perhaps it was the burden of that discontinuity that drove us to cling to metaphysical justice or God's general benevolence or what you will as the meaning of present created life, lest our present life short of the consummation lose all meaning whatever.

But now that Barth has said it, let us take courage and proclaim Jesus Christ, without ambiguity, as the one for whom all things are made and done. Only, lest our former hesitation prove justified, let us be very clear that the unity between life and its consummation in Christ is wrought out in the concrete earthly agony and joy of Jesus' life among us. Let us be clear that Christ's life has *two* sides, death and resurrection, that there is a discontinuity between them which is overcome only by the sequence of His life, and that only so is He the goal of history.

II

How is God related to the history of salvation? Barth answers: God himself is the preeminently historical being; His being and doing are identical. Our history is the cognitive reflection of God's history. Thus God guides the history of salvation in that

He *is* the center of that history; its events are those in which the living God lives. Jesus Christ is the history of God and the history of man at once. Once again it is hard to understand how believers can have hesitated, how they can have used formulations which seem to distinguish a God of timeless pure being from the God at work in Jesus Christ. Yet perhaps that ambiguity resulted from a legitimate concern. Perhaps it resulted from concern that on the one hand Jesus' acts be acts truly performed among us and not somewhere in the bosom of transcendence, and that on the other hand God's transcendence above all the terms of created life be honored.

We will satisfy these concerns if we teach with absolute radicalness of a God who *happens among us* and who preserves His absolute difference from and rule over us precisely by so existing. For it is exactly when God breaks in and acts upon us that we are faced with an Other who resists all our attempts to domesticate Him, whose transcendence is the real thing and not the spurious transcendence of our metaphysical projections. Then also we will be free of the nagging worry—which sometimes we feel in Barth's case—that we may after all be speaking of a different history from that which took place in Palestine and now takes place in our churches.

III

What is it to *be?* Barth answers: It is to have a part to play in Jesus' life story. One more time we will say: Now that it has been said so plainly, it is hard to see how believers can have separated Christ and the creatures made in and for Him by interposing other absolutes, be they ever so gloriously compounded of Truth, Beauty, and Goodness. Yet perhaps they did so lest it seem that

Jesus' life story was not a true history at all, having but one event. Perhaps they drove in these absolutes as wedges to keep God's living history with man, in its three great events of Creation, Reconciliation, and Redemption, from seeming to collapse into one eternal point-event.

We must follow Barth in developing a christological ontology. That is, we must work out a vision of our life and the world we live it in which will be an explication of the Gospel's concrete meaning for the understanding of existence. But lest we fall victim to abstraction and confirm the fear just named, let us stress two points: (1) Christ the eternal incarnate Word *became* flesh. The eternally self-identical Person whose life is the context and basis of our lives lived before He became man, even as He lives eternally as man. It is this progression of His life that is our being. (2) The field of our history and reality is the action of God-in-Christ upon *us*. The confrontation of God-in-Christ with mankind must not be subordinated, for it is this confrontation which makes us real.

IV

Has our "introductory cliché" become less cliché? Let us hope that our discussion with Barth has replaced it with a genuine theological apprehension of Christ as the beginning and end of our destiny. For all Barth's works want only to point to Him, the Alpha and Omega.

SELECTED BIBLIOGRAPHY

A complete bibliography of Karl Barth's works through 1955 is given by Charlotte von Kirschbaum in: *Antwort.* Zurich, 1956, pp. 945–60. Only those works of very particular interest for our subject are included here.

BARTH, KARL. "Die Botschaft von der freien Gnade Gottes." (*Theologische Studien.* No. 23.) Zurich, 1947.

———. *Christ and Adam.* Translated by Smail. New York, 1957. (Original: "Christus und Adam nach Roemer 5." [*Theologische Studien.* No. 35.] Zurich, 1952.)

———. *Die christliche Dogmatik im Entwurf.* Munich, 1927.

———. *Church Dogmatics.* Vol. I/1–IV/3(2) to date. Edinburgh and New York, 1936–. (Original: *Die Kirchliche Dogmatik.* Zurich, 1932–.)

———. *Epistle to the Romans.* Translated by Hoskyns. Oxford, 1933. (Original: *Der Roemerbrief.* 2nd ed. Munich, 1922.)

———."Evangelium und Gesetz." (*Theologische Existenz Heute.* Vol. 32.) 1935.

———. *Fides Quaerens Intellectum.* Translated by Anderson. Richmond, 1960. (Original: *Fides quaerens intellectum.* Munich, 1931.)

———. "Gottes Gnadenwahl." (*Theologische Existenz Heute.* Vol. 47.) 1936.

———. "The Humanity of God." Translated by Thomas. (In: *The Humanity of God.* Richmond, 1960.) (Original: "Die Menschlichkeit Gottes." *Theologische Studien.* No. 48. Zurich, 1956.)

———. *The Knowledge of God and the Service of God according to the Teaching of the Reformation.* London, 1938.

———. *Der Roemerbrief.* 1st ed. Bern, 1919.

———. "Die Wirklichkeit des neuen Menschen." (*Theologische Studien.* No. 27.) Zurich, 1950.

BALTHASAR, URS VON. *Karl Barth.* Cologne, 1951.

BERKOUWER, G. C. *The Triumph of Grace in the Theology of Karl Barth.* Grand Rapids, 1956. (Original: *De triomf der genade in de theologie von Karl Barth.* Kampen, 1954.)

BISSEN, J. M. "La tradition sur la prédestination absolue de Jésus-Christ du VIIe au XIIIe siècle." (*France Franciscaine*. Vol. 22. 1939; pp. 9–34.)

BOUILLARD, HENRI. *Karl Barth*. (In two parts: *Genèse et évolution de la théologie dialectique* and *Parole de Dieu et existence humaine*.) 3 vols. Paris, 1957.

BRUNNER, EMIL. *The Christian Doctrine of God*. Philadelphia, 1950; pp. 229–40, 313–5, 346–53. (Original: *De Christliche Lehre von Gott*. 1959.)

———. "Der neue Barth." (*Zeitschrift fur Theologie und Kirche*. Vol. 48, no. 1. 1951; pp. 89–100.)

BRUNNER, PETER. "Die Freiheit des Menschen in Gottes Heilsgeschichte." (*Kerygma und Dogma*. Vol. 5, no. 3. 1959; pp. 238–57.)

———. "Trennt die Rechtfertigungslehre die Confessionen?" and "Rechtfertigung und Kircheneinheit." (one continued article) (*Zeitwende*. Vol. 30, nos. 8 and 9. 1959; pp. 524–36, 594–608.)

DORNER, I. A. *Entwicklungsgeschichte der Lehre von der Person Christi*. 2 vols. Stuttgart, 1945.

FÉRET, H. M. "Creati in Christo Jesu." (*Revue de les Sciences Philosophiques et Théologiques*. Vol. 1. 1951–2; pp. 96–132.)

GLOEGE, GERHARD. *Barth, Karl*. (In: "Religion in Geschichte und Gegenwart." 3rd ed. Vol. 1, coll. 894–98.)

———. "Zur Praedestinationslehre Karl Barths." (*Kerygma und Dogma*.) Vol. 2, nos. 3, 4. 1956; pp. 193–217, 233–55.)

JENSON, R. W. "Cur Deus Homo? The Election of Christ in the Theology of Karl Barth." Unpublished dissertation. Available from libraries of Heidelberg University and Luther Theological Seminary, St. Paul, Minnesota. 1959.

KÜNG, HANS. "Rechtfertigung. Die Lehre Karl Barths und eine Katholische Besinnung." Paderborn, 1957. (An English version of this monograph is, I understand, in preparation.)

MEZGER, MANFRED. "Gottes Gnadenwahl." (*Verkündigung und Forschung 1947–8*. 1949; pp. 89–96.)

PANNENBERG, WOLFHART. *Dialektische Theologie*. (In: "Religion in Geschichte und Gegenwart." 3rd ed. Vol. 3, coll. 168–74.)

PRENTER, REGIN. "Die Einheit von Schöpfung und Erlösung." (*Theologische Zeitschrift*. Vol. 2, no. 3. 1946; pp. 161–82.)

———. "Die Lehre vom Menschen bei Karl Barth." (*Theologische Zeitschrift*. Vol. 6, no. 3. 1950; pp. 211–22.)

———. *Skabelse og Genløsning*. Copenhagen, 1951; pp. 145–290.

———. "Karl Barths Umbildung der traditionellen Zweinaturlehre in lutherischer Beleuchtung." (*Studia Theologica.* Vol. 11, fasc. 1. 1957; pp. 1–88.)

REID, J. K. "The Office of Christ in Predestination." (*Scottish Journal of Theology.* Vol. 1, nos. 1, 2. 1948.)

SOUCEK, J. B. "Man in the Light of the Humanity of Jesus." (*Scottish Journal of Theology.* Vol. 2, no. 1. 1949; pp. 74–82.)

SPINDELER, ALOYSIUS. *Cur Verbum caro factum?* Paderborn, 1938.

VOGEL, HEINRICH. "Ecce Homo." (*Verkündigung und Forschung 1949–50.* 1951; pp. 102–28.)

VOLK, HERMANN. *Die Christologie bei Karl Barth und Emil Brunner.* (In: "Das Konzil von Chalkedon." Ed. Grillmeier *et al.* 1954. Vol. 3; pp. 613–73.)

WHITEHOUSE, W. A. *Christ and Creation.* (In: "Essays in Christology for Karl Barth." Ed. Parker. London, 1956; pp. 113–32.)

———. "The Nature of Man." (*Scottish Journal of Theology.* Vol. 2, no. 1. 1949; pp. 57–74.)

WINGREN, GUSTAF. "Gott und Mensch bei Karl Barth." (*Studia Theologica.* Vol. 1, fasc. 1, 2. 1948; pp. 27–53.)

———. *Theology in Conflict.* Philadelphia, 1958; pp. 23–44, 108–28. (Original: *Teologiens Metodfraga.* Lund, 1954.)